By **Arthur Edward Waite**
and **Pamela Colman Smith**

TAROT
ORIGINAL 1909

Companion book by **Sasha Graham**

LO SCARABEO

Waite - Smith - Graham
TAROT ORIGINAL 1909

based on the Tarot deck by
Arthur Edward Waite and Pamela Colman Smith
published in December 1909

A book by Sasha Graham

Concept by Arthur Edward Waite
Artwork by Pamela Colman Smith
Text by Sasha Graham
Foreword by Riccardo Minetti
Graphic Layout by Chiara Demagistris
Editing by Elena Delmastro, Riccardo Minetti and Charlie Westby

Printed by Grafiche Stella in August 2021

© Lo Scarabeo
All rights reserved
Via Cigna 110 - 10155 Torino - Italy
info@loscarabeo.com - www.loscarabeo.com
Facebook & Instagram: LoScarabeoTarot

TABLE OF CONTENTS

FOREWORD

Tarot Original 1909. It's probably the most important deck at the present time. With hundreds of new Tarot deck created each year, the one conceived by Arthur Edward Waite and Pamela Colman Smith, still stands as the forefather of them all.

Of course, Tarot did not start in 1909. Documented history brings us back to Milan, in Italy, in the year 1452, with the Visconti Tarot appearing in occasion of the wedding between two important nobles, Francesco Sforza and Bianca Maria Visconti. Legends and theories bring us further back in history, as if going further back in time could bring a purer and more genuine tradition. Truth be told, after 1452 we had to wait a few centuries more before Tarot stopped being used as a card game and started to be used for cartomancy, esotericism and magic. Still, by the XIX century, Tarot had become the "missing link" between the several branches of the western magical tradition: Astrology, Alchemy, Cabballah, just to name a few. And foremost scholars of the occult sciences were striving to unveil the mystery and secrets hidden behind the cards, using the deck that was most famous at that time: the Marseille Tarot.

All this knowledge, all this work, happened to be channeled in a single place and time: London of the first years of the new century, specifically in the fold of the Hermetic Order of the Golden Dawn. Among the members of the Order: Arthur Edward Waite, a writer, scholar and occultist, and Pamela Colman Smith, a young woman and talented artist.

Fate, for those who want to believe in Fate, or coincidence for those who prefer not, further shuffled the cards for the two. In 1907, a full photographic reproduction of a previously undisclosed XV century deck known as the Sola Busca Tarot was donated to the British Museum. Two years later, in the cold December of 1909, the Original 1909 deck was published with just the name of "Tarot" and no other title. Soon after this very first edition, in the early months of 1910, a second edition was released anew, with a different printing technique, more suited to printing large quantities.

Neither Waite, nor Smith, and definitely not the Publisher of that time – a Mr. William Rider – could foresee the influence that unnamed deck would have had in the history and evolution of Tarot.

The greatest innovation and originality of the deck is by far to be found in the Minor Arcana. Contrary to the Tarot of Marseille and most other decks of the past, the Minor Arcana didn't look like playing cards, but were rather illustrated with scenes that referenced the actual meaning of the cards. Just a few years earlier another deck in Italy – the "Naibi di Giovanni Vacchetta" – had done the same thing, but just from an aesthetic and decorative point of view. The scenes of the Major had no reference to their meaning. Likewise, the aforementioned Sola Busca deck, reputed to have been created with strong alchemical influences, had several Minors illustrated, so much that it heavily influenced Pamela's Art for many cards.

Even if these decks predated the Original 1909, they were exceptions and lacked the relevance and the simple powerful charm of this new deck. However, in order to truly understand the depth of the influence and importance of this, we must walk a little further down the river of time and reach the Seventies, when the deck was published anew, albeit not as its first edition. This time the deck had a title, made of the name of one of its authors (it didn't surprise me that – at that time – the name that was omitted was that of Pamela, a woman) and of the original publisher: it was called Rider Waite Tarot.

Earlier in the century, Tarot was – indeed – famous and widespread, its usage was reserved to the scholars (and the charlatans, who never made themselves scarce), who had studied and understood the esoteric meanings and references of the cards. Now, however, Pamela's art in the Minor Arcana opened the interpretation of the cards to everyone. Only one thing was needed: intuition.

Of course, intuition alone had the danger of falling short. Still, with just a little bit of guidance and a good foundation, provided by a single book, intuition was the key to a totally different way of looking at Tarot. Not merely "divination", but a tool for understanding, growth, spiritual guidance…

Arthur and Pamela may have not known it, but they, with that original deck of 1909, had given Tarot life and delivered it in our hands.

As for the good book, the guidance and the solid foundation… my advice is indeed to read Sasha Graham. Yes: this very book as a start.

Riccardo Minetti

CHAPTER ONE

INTRODUCTION

WELCOME

Welcome to the Tarot Original 1909. This deck is reproduced just as it was when released in its First Edition in December 1909. It is the most famous Tarot of the 20th Century. This was the first mass-market Tarot deck to include a companion book with card meanings and detailed, scenic illustrations for the Minor Arcana cards. Artist Pamela Colman Smith's accessible renderings made it possible for anyone to engage in card reading and intuitive divination.

ABOUT THE AUTHORS

Occultist Arthur Edward Waite and artist Pamela Colman Smith belonged to a secret magical society named the Hermetic Order of the Golden Dawn. Its members included theatrical and the intellectual elite drawing the likes of Bram Stoker and William Butler Yeats. The sect used Tarot as a jumping-off point for their mystical operations which included ritual magic, astral travel, scrying, astrological divination, and various occult activities.

ABOUT THE DECK

The Tarot of 1909's symbolism and occult influence draws from Freemasonry, Alchemy, Rosicrucianism, Egyptian iconography, Hebraic Cabbalah, the Tree of Life, and older historical Tarot decks. Christian symbolism is woven through the deck because Waite and Smith both came from Christian backgrounds.

ABOUT READING TAROT

Using Tarot is simple. Ask a question. Flip a card. Gaze at the image. Tell the story of what you see. The more you study and practice, the deeper you will go. The better you will become. Tarot works differently for every individual because no two people are alike. Each of us have unique gifts, sensibilities, and intentions. Tarot's effectiveness depends on who uses it and how they use it. You will learn to cultivate your own unique reading style.

CHAPTER TWO

TAROT BASICS

HOW A TAROT READING WORK

Reading Tarot isn't difficult. There are a few elements involved, and the better they are done individually, the better is the complete reading experience. These elements are:
– Shuffling the deck
– Asking a question
– Lay out the cards into a Spread
– Interpret the cards' meanings

SHUFFLING AND HANDLING THE DECK

The point of shuffling is to mix the cards. It should be done between readings in any way that suits you. Mix the cards face down on the table, cut them in your hands, or thumb shuffle like a casino dealer. Infuse your cards with intention by thinking about what you would like to know as you shuffle. Shuffling clears the mind and set the stage for the gathering of information that is to come.

Place the stack of shuffled cards before you. Turn the cards from left to right like opening a page of a book. Decide whether or not you want anyone else to touch the cards. Some feel others disturb the energetic connection they foster with their deck. Other readers want their seeker's energy to fill the deck. The choice is up to you.

QUESTIONS

You'll receive good answers from Tarot when you ask a good question. It helps a reading move smoothly. It results in crystal clear answers from the deck. Smart questions encourage your brain to find the solutions. Be sure to include two elements:

1. Acknowledge the role you play in your future.

2. State your desired outcome.

Examples: Avoid *why* and *will* questions. Ask *how* and *what* questions instead. Instead of asking "Why can't I find love?" Ask the cards "What can I do to find love?" Instead of asking, "Why am I broke?" Rephrase the question into, "What can I do to save more money?" Instead of asking "Will I be happy?" Rephrase into, "What can I focus on to bring happiness into my life?"

SPREADS

Tarot spreads are card layouts where the card position holds a particular meaning.

Past/Present/Future Spread is an excellent beginning spread: you can start from here. Ask a question and layout three cards.

1. Past: What happened in the past.
2. Present: The energy around you now.
3. Future: Most likely outcome.

Once you become proficient, you can insert any number of card attributions for nuanced information. Here are three different "triplets" that can be useful to answer different kinds of questions.

Questions related to interiority, understanding, and personal growth:
1. Hindsight — **2.** Insight — **3.** Foresight

Questions related to problems to be solved or objectives to be reached:
1. Desire — **2.** Challenge — **3.** Solution

Questions related to relationships and love:
1. Me Alone — **2.** You Alone — **3.** Us Together

Questions related to choices and decisions:
1. Don't Do This — **2.** Situation — **3.** Do This

TAROT INTERPRETATION

Don't worry about getting a card's meaning wrong. You know more than you think you do. Read the Tarot as you would read a graphic novel or a simple comic strip. Observe the illustrations. What is happening on each card? Use the image to create a story. Let the story offer a message that applies to your question. Go with your first instincts. Trust yourself. What are the characters doing? Where is the energy moving? What symbols leap to your attention? All of these elements can inform your reading. Trust what comes up for you. Feel the gentle whispers of intuition and let it guide you.

REVERSALS

This is an optional technique. Reversals are cards appearing upside down from your point of view. It is important to decide how you will read reversals before casting your cards. Reversals can be read in multiple ways:

1. Ignore the reversal, turn the card right-side up.

2. Use a reversal keyword.

3. Reversal indicates a blockage of card energy or a delay in time.

4. Reversal is a card asking for special attention.

5. A reversal is the opposite of the card's upright meaning.

UNDERSTANDING TAROT

While there are many different Tarot decks in the world, they all share some common characteristics. Tarot is – at the same time – all the possible and theoretical Tarot decks, and the specific deck in your hands. The first may provide you with context and perspective, while the second will be the deck you actually use for reading.

TAROT'S STRUCTURE

Tarot is divided into the Major Arcana and Minor Arcana. Arcana means "secrets." The secret of the Arcana is that – you already know what they mean. You just might not know that you know them. Until now.

The Major Arcana are archetypal images. Psychologist Carl Jung defines archetype as universally understood concepts. An archetype is an idea or thing that anyone, anywhere can understand no matter their culture or upbringing. For instance, the Fool is the "outsider." The Magician is a "sorcerer." The Empress is a "mother." The Emperor is a "father" and so on. The Major Arcana represents important events and soul evolution.

The Minor Arcana contains the "small secrets" indicative of daily life and moment-to-moment experiences. Minors are identified with a single Roman numeral and no title (except for the Court Cards who carry a royal title but no number). Minors are assigned to the four suits, numbered 1-10, plus the Court Cards.

TAROT'S STRUCTURE

MAJORS

PENTACLES   SWORDS

CUPS   WANDS

NUMERALS

MINORS

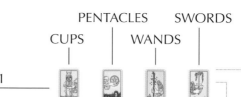

	CUPS	PENTACLES	WANDS	SWORDS
1				
2				
3				
4				
5				
6				
7				
8				
9				
10				
PAGE				
KNIGHT				
QUEEN				
KING				

COURTS

TAROT SUITS

Tarot's four suits provide context and meaning for interpretation. The four suits align with the four elements.

WANDS				FIRE
SWORDS				AIR
CUPS				WATER
PENTACLES				EARTH

Wands align with the element of Fire. Wands are hot like summer. Wands reflect energy and passion. Wands reflect work, career and business. Wands are intentions and personal calling. Wands are drive and excitement. Wands reflect erotic sensuality. Wands light the path toward our destiny. A Wand symbol is a staff. Green leaves fall from the Wand to signify manifestation.

Swords align with the element of Air. Swords are fast-moving. Swords are thoughts, ideas, and mental activities. They are the stories we tell ourselves and the stories we tell others. Swords are the narratives. Swords are all forms of communication, written, verbal, and unspoken. A Sword is a sharp and pointed weapon used to impale or defend. Swords reflect two sides of any issue.

Cups align with the element of Water. The world of Cups is fluid. Cups are emotional. Cups are feelings like happiness, pain, and everything in-between. Cups reflect art and imagination. Cups are dreaming and psychic ability. A Cup symbol is deep and yielding. Cups contain, hold, and nurture.

Pentacles align with the element of Earth. The world of Pentacles feels like a fall harvest. Pentacles are slow but stable. Pentacles represent everything you can touch, taste, see, and feel. Pentacles are things such as property, cars, and belongings. Pentacles are money and resources. Pentacles represent the material world. Pentacles show us how to grow and evolve. A Pentacle symbol is a five pointed magical star inside a circle.

Fire/Wands = Action/Passion/Career
Air/Swords = Thoughts/Communication/Words
Water/Cups = Feelings/Emotions/Love
Earth/Pentacles = Material/Things/Money

NUMBERS

Minor Arcana numbers are help understand how to interpret the cards. It is easier than you might think. Every story has a beginning, middle, end, and so does each suit. Aces or ones are the beginning of the story. Aces signify a new cycle, idea, or beginning. The middle of a story is where the challenging part comes in. Tarot fives present a challenge or weighty issue. Tens represent the end of a cycle. The remaining numbers fall in between.

1. One = Beginning
2. Two = Partnership
3. Three = Creativity
4. Four = Structure
5. Five = Challenge
6. Six = Heart Expansion
7. Seven = Uncanny
8. Eight = Infinite Perfection
9. Nine = Wish Fulfillment
10. Ten = Ending

COURT CARDS

Each suit contains a King, Queen, Page, and Knight. The Court Cards are identified by their title. Break the Courts into a family structure remember what they mean.

Page/Daughter = Child: awareness and curiosity.

Knight/Son = Teen: bursting energy.

Queen/Mother = Mature female: compassion and nurturing.

King/Father = Mature masculine: control and structure.

Court card environments match their suits. Wands court cards are set in a hot, dusty, desert environment. Swords are set on airy, breezy mountaintops with Swords. Cups are set near aquatic landscapes. Pentacles are set in garden environments.

All the Knights ride a horse. They are heralds of their suit, bringing messages and forging communication. Read the energy of your situation by paying attention to the gait of the horse and the direction in which they are moving in.

Court Cards will appear in readings to represent people you know. They can be your mother, father or boyfriend or best friend. They can represent co-workers or teachers and people who are about to come into your life. Court Cards can be you and your personality. The Queen of Cups is full of empathy and reflects you as a confidant. Court Cards can suggest an attitude. For example, you ask how to get a work promotion. The Queen of Swords appears. She is direct and to the point. Her advice is to ask for exactly what you want.

YOUR TAROT JOURNAL

Tarot journals are wildly helpful as Tarot is a personal experience. Make a unique list of keywords, intuitions, and ideas about Tarot. Track your readings, spreads, and messages. Record a single card at a time with one dedicated page for each card. Include two or three keywords from this book. Gaze at the card and write down mental associations. Make a list of the symbols. What do the symbols mean to you? How does the energy of the card feel? Sketch the card. Write short stories about them. No one sees the world like you do. No one else will read Tarot like you.

TABLE FOR TAROT JOURNAL

Here are a few things you may find useful to mark in your Tarot journal. Noting some down, like the Card Name, will help your memory, while other entries will gather your progressive insights in a card, and help you make them consistent.

– Card Name
– Major/Minor/Court
– Keywords
– Associations
– Energy
– Colors
– Number
– Symbols
– Symbols Associations
– Short Stories/Poetry
– Sketches

CHAPTER THREE

THE MAJOR ARCANA

0. THE FOOL

Hero

"A fresh beginning."

Key: Outsider, Potential, Foolishness, Innocence, Euphoria, Journey.
Reversed: Delinquent, Pretentious.

The Fool walks in pure optimism bringing life and possibility with him. He represents unfolding consciousness and ripe possibilities inside you. You won't know what's possible until you take the first step. He is potential manifesting into the material world. He does not think ahead of himself or place judgments on the world around him. The Fool marks a brand new cycle and the ultimate fresh start. Everything begins again with freshness. You are in a new place. An ocean of opportunity flows at your fingertips.

The Fool is a clearinghouse of the senses. He is perception, feeling, and experience. He is the way in which he individual organizes the world inside the body. The Fool looks at the world in pure innocence and without predetermined labels. Doing so, he is free to experience the reality before him. He never tires of looking, seeing, and observing because the world is continually new in his eyes.

The Fool is the first card of the Original 1909 deck. The number zero connects the Fool to the World card, acting as a clasp between the end and the beginning of a cycle. He is the heart of flow. He tells you not to question, just go with what's happening. The Fool is not a simpleton but a creature in search of stimulation and adventure. He is the soul in search of experience. What lay in wait for you?

The Fool's cap sprouts a red feather and is found in ancient versions of the Fool card. Throughout antiquity, feathers were used as symbols of immortality. The Fool, Death, and the Sun card each portray a red feather. The symbol strings a soul's evolution from the beginning, into the middle, and to the end of their journey.

Ten circles appear on the Fool's shirt. The circles represent the ten Sephiroth on the Cabbaistic Tree of Life. Each circle connects to the Minor Arcana beginning from the ace at the top to the ten at the bottom. A careful examination of the circles reveals an eight-spoke wheel inside each circle. Just as the star inside a pentacle represents the four elements conjoined with the human spirit, the eight-spoke wheel is a Golden Dawn symbol for Spirit.

The Fool stands at the precipice of a cliff. Does he see the danger before him? The secret of the card is that he is safe. The path regenerates with each step. It is a reminder for you to trust your path. The dog is the animating principle of life and a loyal friend. The Fool's bag contains your previous experience. It is collecting and keeping only the habits and lessons that serve you so you can begin anew.

I. MAGICIAN

Sorcerer or Sorceress
"You are the magic."

Key: Mastery, Confidence, Talent, Will, Charisma.
Reversed: Anxiety, Slander, Devious

The Magician appears in readings to mark personal achievement, the ability to wow a crowd, and being the object of attention. You fascinate others. On stage, you are pure presence. You are putting on a show and receiving the attention you deserve. This card is an excellent omen for mastery, displaying prowess, and winning over the opinions of others. The Magician ignites the Tarot with electricity. He reflects how you fill your life with energy and intention. Wild charisma charms the audience but the Magician asks you to look deeper. How can you achieve your ultimate goal?

The Magician shows you how to use energy and magic. The Magician's posture holds dual meanings. His magic wand points up while the other hand points to the earth. We see in his posture how to siphon energy. We are all lightning rods of vitality. His stance shows us how inspiration moves through us and into any person, place, or thing we put our attention on. We "light up," what we focus on, thus, the power of our attention.

The Magician tells you, "As above, so below." This occultist's saying is simple and elegant. What is true for the universe (the macrocosm) is true for you (microcosm). Earth is a reflection of heaven. You are a reflection of the divine. What is true for the invisible world is also true in the visible. What exists inside of you, your intimate, interior world composed of thoughts, ideas, and feelings also exists on the outside. When you feel sad, the entire world feels dour and depressing. When you are happy, the world feels delightful. As above, so below.

"As above, so below," aligns with the knowledge that what you feel, know, and imagine is what you make real in the world. You will recall how every single invention from the wheel to the Internet was once invisible. It was once an idea, a fantasy in someone's head. This principle aligns with Laws of Attraction, which says what you focus on is what you bring into your life.

The infinity symbol appears as a horizontal figure eight (*lemniscate*). It matches the magician's vertical stance. The nature of infinity is echoed in the Magician's belt. It is a snake eating its own tail. Each symbol represents the boundless nature of the universe.

Four items sit on the Magician's table. They each align with the four suits of Tarot and thus the four elements: a Sword (Air/Thoughts), Cup (Water/Feelings), Pentacle (Earth/Things), and Wand (Fire/Energy). This is a reminder that everything you need is always before you. What will you do with what's right in front of you? This becomes your magic.

The Magician is an energetic channel for three-fold levels of existence, the upper spiritual world (divinity), the middle world of reality (the one we all live in), and the lower world (shadow). The blooming roses and lilies represent abundant, fruitfulness against the luminous yellow energy of the sun that the Fool has carried with him.

II. HIGH PRIESTESS

Inner Self
"Blueprint of the soul."

Key: Oracle, Occult, Enigma, Authenticity, Mystery, Intelligence.
Reversed: Weakness, Shallow.

The High Priestess is everything making you "You". She is your deepest secrets, even those you hide from yourself. She appears in readings to remind you of your soul's origin story. Who are you in the truest sense? Quiet yourself to hear whispers of truth. She helps you find the words only you can say.

The High Priestess reminds you that you hold the answer to any question you might ask the cards or the universe. Waite calls her the "highest and holiest" of all the Arcana because she is the secret to who you are. She reminds you to check in with yourself. She is stillness and silence. Find these qualities before proceeding in your situation. There is no one else who can answer this but you.

The High Priestess suggests there is no action required other than showing up and being present. It is important to exert our influence or make our needs known at times. But when the High Priestess appears, she says sit back with her knowing smile. Let things play out without asserting your impulses and opinion. You'll be surprised to see the situation resolve itself on its own. Sometimes, being passive is the most active thing you can do.

High Priestess symbolism is rich and complex. She sits between two pillars, one black and one white to reflect duality. Her figure is the integration of polarities thus reflecting how we are always combining opposing forces in our life. We surf through our days from wakefulness to sleep, from our high to low. We move between work and rest and integrate our masculine and feminine sides. We are always somewhere between the two. The pillars bear the initials J and B, a secret of Freemasonry. The letters stand for Jachin and Boaz who are the names of the two pillars on King Solomon's temple, in Jerusalem. Masonic rituals are linked to rites, stories, and allegories of Solomon's Temple. The pillars were described as 27 feet tall, which would make the High Priestess on this card a massive 25-foot tall figure.

The High Priestess holds a scroll with the Hebrew word TORA on it. TORA means "teachings" or "doctrines." This sacred scroll is the book of your life. It is where you came from, why you are here - what will happen after you depart. It is the key of who you are. It cannot be read, it must be lived. The end is a mystery no one can see.

III. EMPRESS

Mother

"The expansion of your creative soul."

Key: Nurturing qualities, Plentiful, Activity, Originality, Fertility, Reinvention.
Reversed: Doubt, Impotent.

The Empress is all creativity and expression. She appears in readings as the mother archetype to suggest the nurturing, beauty, and sensuality thriving inside you. She reflects the best part of you when you take care of yourself and others. Her advice is to use your creativity for the situation at hand. You might surprise yourself with solutions when you think out of the box.

If the High Priestess reflects your internal resources and basic design, it is the Empress who colors the design of you. She sets everything free. She is the flower shoot seeking sunlight, the artist meeting the canvas. She is pure desire and expressive passion. She is love and instinct. The Empress is sunshine in the morning and the purple twilight of evening. She reflects the creative process and pure femininity.

The Empress births your High Priestess secrets into the earthly world. She is you brimming with potentialities, talents, and deliciousness. Her scepter represents the globe of the world. You hold the world in your hand. It is yours to do with what you like. How will you use your power and finesse?

Harmony and pleasure are at the forefront of the Empress. How can you bring more of each to your life? If you are struggling with a thorny situation, the Empress suggests finding equilibrium quickly. Apply pleasure and kindness to smooth over rough spots. What small adjustments will bring physical pleasure? How can simplicity breed desire? Stop overthinking things. The answer is clear and simple.

The symbol of Venus on her shield connects her to beauty and sensuality. The string of white pearls around her neck, her velvet pillows, and robes all contain symbols of Venus, goddess of love and pleasure. Her field of wheat is sacred to ancient corn goddesses and Greek Grain Mother Demeter. The silent reaping of an ear of corn was a central symbol to the Greek Eleusinian mysteries. Grain and wheat are cross-cultural symbols of new life. The twelve stars on her crown reflect the twelve signs of the zodiac and mark her as the queen of the universe.

The Empress is usually portrayed as pregnant beneath her robes. This metaphorical pregnancy extends to all things you are creating in your life. It speaks to the family you may someday create to the projects you undertake. It reminds you of your power as a creative being. There is nothing you can't do if you believe in yourself.

Ultimately, this archetype reminds you of your own magnificence in the world. It is your power of reinvention and the ability to make anything fresh and new by changing your approach. She will appear to represent mother figures in your life. The Empress can represent the negative or dark side of unresolved mother issues when reversed. She sometimes appears to foretell a physical pregnancy.

IV. EMPEROR

Father
"Setting boundaries."

Key: Structure, Steadfast, Dependable, Command, Conviction, Purpose.
Reversed: Difficulty, Trapped.

The Emperor is the part of you that creates habit and form. He is the way you structure your day, organize your work, and create a foundation. He is the systems – or lack of system you employ to get things done. The Emperor is the glue that holds together the universe and gives it form and shape. The Emperor is the atomic molecules. He is Newton's rules, Einstein's physics. He is how weather forms and how the atmosphere keeps air on our planet. While the Empress represents expansion and creation, it is the Emperor who puts everything in its place. Without the Emperor, life would be a continual series of never endings Big Bangs.

His number four is a building block of the universe. Think of a brick, a table, or a chair. Anything solid that must create support has four corners. This is the essence of the Emperor. He is the support you place down in order to hold everything you need.

The Emperor places limits on our consciousness. The Emperor is the structure where habits are formed and broken. Though he appears intimidating, he is flexible in that you always have the ability to alter and move your boundaries. He reflects the narrative structure and the way we form thoughts. He gives you the power to change your thoughts. He is like the binding structure of Tarot and archetype.

The Emperor is the archetype of the father. He often appears to represent "dad issues." This is the way you have responded to the father figures in your life. It can mark the way you act fatherly or exert fatherly influence towards others. The Emperor often appears to represent an authority figure or influential person who can help you advance in your goals.

The Emperor holds an Egyptian ankh in his right hand, which represents immortality. This Egyptian symbol deconstructs into the rising sun (the circle at the top of the cross) and/or the union of the male and female energies. It is the union of opposites. Aries the ram rules the Emperor. Four rams appear on the Emperor's throne. The Emperor's crown has ram horns sprouting from the top. The Emperor's robes are vibrant red, the color of Mars, Aries' ruling planet.

The Golden Dawn gave the Emperor the esoteric function of "Sight." He is the way you look at the world. No one else sees the world you see. Life, although a shared experience, is ultimately your own intimate experience. The further you gaze, the more will become available to you. The Emperor appears to remind you to seek new horizons each day.

V. HIEROPHANT

Spiritual Advisor
"Sacred secrets."

Key: Teaching, Mentorship, Religion, Dogma, Sacrament, Guidance, Ritual.
Reversed: Distrust, Skepticism.

The Hierophant reveals secrets and mysteries of the unseen world. The Hierophant appears to us in the form of nun, priest, rabbi, or shaman. They exist as outer symbols to let us know mystery is real. Hierophants reflect the attempt to explain and understand deep, spiritual mysteries. He is all forms of religion and laws in regular life. He is the holy books, psalms, and sermons. He is the external form of church, temple, and ritualistic meeting place. He is scripture and dogma, incense, and prayer.

The Hierophant often appears to represent cultural norms, especially those systems we brush up against when we don't fit into them. The Hierophant generally speaks to and for the masses. He represents the way in which rules and dogma are used for control and manipulation. He is group think.

The Hierophant might reveal the way you have clashed or disagree with religious systems. He also represents the beauty of ritual and sacred space. He can be the solace you have found in shared ideas of divinity. The Hierophant card reflects student and teacher or the master and disciple relationship. It is how you inhabit both roles and what these relationships mean to you.

A graphic triad is formed within the card with the Hierophant at the upper centre. Two monks stand before the Hierophant with their heads in tonsure. Tonsure is the act of shaving one's head to display religious devotion. A commonplace practice in medieval times. A "w" is found on top of the Hierophant's crown. This letter can also stand for the initial of Waite's name. The Taurus symbol, a circle with a crescent moon shape above it, can be seen hidden upon the Hierophant's throne. A circle with a dot in the center is seen on each side of the Hierophant's head. It is the symbol for alchemist's gold.

White lilies decorate the right monk's clothing while red roses mark the left monk. These same flowers are found inside the Magician card. The crossed keys unlock dogmatic secrets. They remind you Tarot itself is a key that will unlock the mysteries of both you and the universe. The Hierophant makes the sign of benediction with his right hand, also seen in the Devil card. A triple staff is seen in the Hierophant's left hand marking the upper, middle, and lower worlds. The Hierophant bears multiple visual similarities to the High Priestess. They each sit between two pillars and wear a triple crown. She reflects the secrets of you while he reflects the spiritual secrets of the universe and how they can be understood.

VI. LOVERS

Romance
"Falling in love."

Key: Choice, Seduction, Allure, Desire, Eroticism.
Reversed: Repulsion, Abandon.

The Lovers card is falling in love and languishing in the flames of desire. It is erotic attraction and excitement. It represents hot and heavy romance. The mad chemical dopamine rush of ecstasy and excitement rush through you at the beginning of a new relationship. Your cheeks flush fever hot, a single gaze sends waves of longing through your body. It is warm breath, the brush of a fingertip. It is the object of your desire as a magical, tantric experience as if crafted by the gods themselves.

The card depicts Adam and Eve but it is also Romeo and Juliet, Eros and Psyche, Samson and Delilah, Tristan and Isolde. Two souls become one. It is the act of love. The couple stands naked amidst the fruit trees and foliage of the Garden of Eden. They are anointed by an angel who hovers above them. A clever snake observes them.

We can take the Lovers at face value and take it at face value. A pair of Lovers, a hook up, a good time. But if we scratch the surface and gaze deeper we examine love not simply as the binding quality of the universe but also the ability to be intimate with something or someone. To hold them close with complete vulnerability. Consider the sexual implications of this card. Consensual acts of love are healing and expressive or can be destructive and cruel.

The Lovers card appears to signify love in your life but it also appears as an invitation to open yourself up to love in all its aspects. The Lovers are a metaphysical reminder that we are not confined by our physical body. Lovers evoke the most potent force known in the universe. Our physical, biological, and spiritual goals are expressed in this card. It is fire, fury and passion, the point of human existence. It is the source of manifestation. Love is the source of all life.

Forty-five sun rays stream from behind archangel Raphael, angel of healing. His presence exudes the restorative properties of love to the couple below. Raphael's hair is aflame as fiery as the sun behind him and the flaming tree below. Fire elements express elements of desire. The snake is a symbol of temptation and also reflects an occultist moving up the Tree of Life. A distant mountain peak foretells the heights possible for the Lovers as well as the occultist's spiritual ascent. Clouds appear below the angel to express divine manifestation as in all of the Aces. The man gazes toward the female who looks up at the angel who peers down upon all. This marks the triangular energy of the ultimate creative act.

VII. CHARIOT

Hero
"Being in the driver's seat."

Key: Moving forward with confidence, Aid, Battle, Pride, Conquest, Agility.
Reversed: Collapse, Breakdown, Wait.

It is time to forge ahead. The Chariot is where gifts, intentions, and passions are brought out and put to use in the world. The individual strives, moves and dares greatly. You are taking action. Your plan is made, your intentions are clear. This is the time. It's now or never. Make your move. Take ownership of the vehicle. Chart your course and start moving.

The Chariot is made of a cube of stone too large for its golden wheels. Why would the Chariot, the symbol of speed, movement, and military prowess be placed on a heavy, immobile object? The answer lays in the level of existence the Chariot represents. Psychologist Jung sees the Chariot as a symbol of the self. Spiritual movement is paramount, the ultimate goal of the esoteric. Therefore, a person could travel the world in a literal sense but never see beneath its surface. They can remain spiritually starved or stuck. It is why the Chariot remains immobile outside of city walls.

Waite describes the Chariot as "princely" but not "heredity royalty and not a priest." Waite reveals the Chariot's true nature unequivocally, "He is above all things triumph in the mind." It suggests you have decided upon success and nothing less. It is the attitude of already having won or achieved your goal. The function of the Chariot is as the driver of your personal will.

The Chariot is an actor of the physical world yet he is draped in esoteric symbolism. His shoulder pates are the profile faces of "Urim and Thummim". They are figures that appear in the Book of Exodus and are connected to divination. Priests used them for divination (yes, you read that correctly). In 1827, Joseph Smith, founder of the Mormon sect used two seer stones called Urim and Thummim to write the Book of Mormon. Interestingly, Joseph Smith, a Freemason, used Masonic structure to craft Mormon rituals, the same way the Golden Dawn used Masonic structure to organize their own grades and esoteric work.

The esoteric function of the Chariot is "Speech." Inside this card lay the power of your words. Words carry knowledge and intention, two vastly powerful qualities. Words have the power to imprint the mind. To speak an intention is to take one step closer to making your goal or desire real. Barriers are expressed by the high wall enclosing the city behind and the Chariot's battle armor. The astrological association of the Chariot is Cancer who's symbol is a crab. A hard outer shell protects this crustacean's soft body. It is like the shell of the Charioteer's vehicle and armor. Cancer is ruled by the moon. The Chariot's belt holds five symbols. Two of them are the astrological symbols for Moon. The sphinxs' black and white colors match the High Priestess's black and white pillars. It is the way in which you combine opposing energies to direct your course and chart your way.

VIII. STRENGTH

Fortitude
"Power of finesse."

Key: Dynamic, Vitality, Discipline, Vigor, Victory.
Reversed: Corruption, Disrespect.

The Strength card marks physical, emotional, and intellectual fortitude. It appears in a reading to remind you of the stamina you possess. Strength is the quality needed to meet each and every challenge in life. It is always present and keenly felt and tested in times of uncertainty. Strength fosters possibility and stability. Strength appears inside moral fibers and in the decisions and actions set in the habits of your life.

The Strength figure expresses kindness to her animal friend and strength is shown in the way we treat ourselves and those around us. It includes animals, people, and our environment. Traditionally, the Strength cards show a female taming a wild lion. The Original 1909 card reflects a lion that has already been tamed. The beast is putty in her hands. It reflects the maintenance of strength, not the struggle for it. It is the pen, which is mightier than the sword. It is charm and prowess rather than brute force.

Strength marks contemplative practices such as meditation. This is the practice of quieting the mind. The first step is to become aware of thoughts and letting them drift without becoming attached to them. It allows us to see the transient nature of life and thinking. We learn to respond to the world around us rather than react to it. This is how we tame our inner lion.

The Golden Dawn switched Strength with the traditional placement of the Justice card to align with cabbalistic and astrological attributions. Waite tells about the flowers which strength wears as, "among many other things, the sweet yoke and the light burden of Divine Law." The "sweet yoke" Waite speaks of is the link between you and divine creativity.

The lion is symbolic of astrological Leo. This same symbol appears in the Wheel of Fortune's lower left corner. The lemniscate above the female's head is also seen above the Magician. It marks the infinite nature of energy, life, and the divine. The rising mountain in the distance suggests spiritual heights and the unfolding journey of the following cards.

Strength appears to remind you that Strength simmers with constant power to illuminate everything. It is causality itself. Strength is the inner reserves of power wielded in profound gestures. It is intellectual, physical, and emotional fortitude. It is exuding tenacity of character, personal responsibility, and inner confidence no matter the external circumstance.

Elder

"Luminous interior knowledge."

Key: Sagacity, Vigilance, Divine Mystery, Introversion, Retreat.
Reversed: Fright, Hiding.

The Hermit appears as a reminder to pull away from the influence of others. It is time to strike your own path. It is the examination of personal nature and individual sensate experience. Existence is a subjective experience. We are the only ones who feel it for ourselves. Spiritual and sensual nature is one and the same. It is the way the world enters our body. Each one of us is different. The Hermit is that place we go to time and time again to check in with ourselves. It is the place we discover what can't be described by anyone else.

The Hermit sequesters herself to hear the divine whispers of the universe. Recorded knowledge provides groundwork but only each individual can experience their unique relationship with the unseen. This is why esoteric scholars and soul seekers value seclusion. It is the point of a vow of silence. In profound fecundity of silence and darkness we become the active observer. We respond to the living universe and the nature of who we are. Away from noise, sound, and distraction we can detect the innermost trembling of our soul. This is why Hermits seek vast deserts and deep caves. It is a safe space to examine the nature your soul far and away from the psychic energy of others.

Our regular daily life is an energy exchange. We are all, in a sense, energetic vampires. Each of us are empaths and caregivers. We continually engage in energetic give and take, which is not a bad thing. Human connection and shared experience feel good to us. It keeps us connected to others. Yet, inside this connection, amidst the noise of everyday life, it can be hard to cultivate internal energy or even find a sense of stillness.

Time alone feeds the soul. It fosters discovery and wisdom. We evolve as we act in line with the truth of who we are. We grow when we remember what was forgotten. The Hermit gives us a place to encounter his spiritual sister the High Priestess. He is our doorway to her threshold. The first ten cards of the Original 1909 deck described the process by which we become human. It is evolution of the psyche and the self. Once we are complete, the Hermit uses his lamp to guide us home.

The six-pointed star inside his lantern is a universal symbol of hope. The Hermit displays inspiration and guidance from the top of a mountain. His staff, also carried by the Fool and the Eight of Cups, is what he uses to make his ascent. The mountain peak on which the Hermit stands reflects spiritual height. Recall how many mountain tops are visible throughout the deck. Snow covered mountain peaks further conveys the altitudes, which mark your heightened awareness. The Hermit's beard denotes the wisdom of age and is also found on the older gentleman in the Ten of Pentacles. The Hermit's head covering is a sign of devotion and respect of spiritual power residing above.

X. WHEEL OF FORTUNE

Revolution

"Time is on your side."

Key: Fortune, Fame, Happiness, Lucky Turn, Winds of Fate.
Reversed: Out of alignment.

The Wheel of Fortune shows up to inform us our luck is about to change for the better. The winds of fate blow kindly upon our backs. This lucky omen reminds us of the Latin proverb that fortune favors the bold. We must jump into life; play the hand we are dealt, and take an active role in order to dance with our destiny.

The Wheel of Fortune is a symbol of cosmic momentum. It echoes our life cycles, the sunrises, siestas, and sunsets. It is decades, months, seconds, and each moment breeds possibility.

Time is linear yet pliable. We move between inner and outer time and find we can bend it. Outer time belongs to the clock and calendar. Inner time is reflected by an imagination capable of recalling any moment of our life. Deep time occurs as we become one with the present moment in the immersion of the World card.

The Wheel of Fortune can be a useful contemplation tool like a Buddhist mandala or Hindu chakra wheel marking the nature of time, life, and reality. Arthur Waite explains, "the symbolic picture stands for the perpetual motion of a fluid universe and for the flux of human life." The revolution of the entire solar system is contained within the image.

The wheel spins and a snake slithers down while the jackal cycles up. A mysterious sphinx enjoys the fleeting view. The revolving wheel is cycles of luck, the ups and downs in life. The only way to keep equilibrium is to find your center point.

The word "Rota" is Latin for wheel and placed to read like the phonetic "Tarot." The spokes are the three alchemical symbols of Mercury, Sulfur, and Salt. The astrological symbol of Aquarius is found above the "R." Clouds billow in the four corners and like the aces reflect the manifestation of something new in the material world.

Traces of divinity are made manifest in the corners. Four creatures representing a biblical Tetramorph as found in the first chapter of Ezekiel decorate the card. They are the head of a man (Mathew the Apostle), lion (Mark the Evangelist), ox (Luke the Evangelist) and eagle (John the Evangelist). Naturally, the four corner creatures align with the four suits of Tarot.

This is a powerful card churning at the heart center of the Major Arcana. It marks the progression of cards moving from the physical plane where each card denotes a life lesson to the advancement of spiritual lessons. The Wheel of Fortune is a foreshadowing of the World card. This card is the hinge upon which your entire world will change. Do you sense it? Can you feel it?

It is the ultimate reminder that we are each the center of our own unique universe. People we love, situations we encounter, cycles of life revolve in and around us. People move into our orbit, sometimes close, and other times far. The only thing that is certain is that we are all part of a cosmic interplay of time and space.

XI. JUSTICE

Law
"Be firm and be fair."

Key: Karma and rules of society, Integrity, Work, Righteous, Truth.
Reversed: Favoritism, Legal Blockage.

The Justice card reflects work, effort, and karma. It is the witch's rule of three. The energy you put out returns to you times three, often more. This applies to everything from your career to your relationships. This card reminds you to take responsibility for whom you are and the energy you put into the world.

We test the personal limits of Justice often when we are young. It is natural to test what we can get away with when authority figures give us rules and boundaries. Justice is the place we consider and weigh our personal actions, entanglements, and to hone our inner compass. How does it feel to get away with something that was cruel, selfish or mean? We discover there are always ramifications. Doing the right thing can be a scary choice. Showing up when you would rather run in the opposite direction takes strength and courage. Yet, we discover it pays off in spades.

Justice is the logic inherent in the material world and all that comes with it. In obvious ways, it represents courts, laws, and public systems of justice. It is order keeping and controlling societal chaos. Justice is literal law in motion such as the settling of contracts, police, security and all legal matters.

Tarot's Justice wears no blindfold. She sees all as she holds a scale in the right hand, a sword in the left. The posture gently echoes the Magician. Justice's left forefinger points toward the ground as if to channel energy. The figure sits between two pillars like the High Priestess. Justice integrates all sides of a story delicately balancing the nature of truth.

The Justice card connects to the natural talents we are born with. It reminds you that your inherent gifts are divinely influenced. Who gets what and why – it's mystery that will never be solved. Waite tells us talents are like "fairy gifts." We can let out gifts guide us but we have the choice to show up for what we love, regardless of natural talent. Intrinsic talent will never take the place of dedication, focus, and diligence.

The Justice card appears to remind you to let your gifts guide you. We find what we are meant for in this world and the scales of Justice are balanced as we settle into the alignment of who we are. This is why the card echoes the High Priestess. The Justice card is what you do with what you've been given. It is also how your choices affect the world and those around you.

XII. HANGED MAN

Mystic

"Ability to see the situation from a new perspective."

Key: Watchfulness, Offering, Mystic, Occultism, Prophecy.
Reversed: Common thinking, Crowd psychology.

The Hanged Man dangles upside down by his foot but he is anything but still and complacent. The gift of the Hanged Man is the ability to look directly through your current situation. It is the ability to see things from an entirely different perspective. This is the card of mystics and artists. His gift to you is the ability to tossing aside preconceived notions so you can see the world with a fresh pair of eyes.

He appears in your readings to remind you to stop and pay attention to what's right in front of you. Hanged Man advice is to pause and wait before rushing ahead. Pause your normal routine. He peers deeply into the nature of your soul. The artist sees a world no one else can see. They express it in their work. The author imagines new worlds and perspectives and writes them into existence. The composer arranges the notes to an orchestra can bring an audience to new musical territory. The visionary leads people on a path to freedom. What do you see that no one else can see? How will you free yourself?

The stasis of the man occurs only from the outsider's perspective. The Hanged Man's internal life pulsates and moves. Look through his kaleidoscopic eyes. It is like taking a psychedelic drug. The trees whisper, walls bleed color; crickets scratch your skin with song. Senses come alive as predetermined definitions fade back into human memory. A forest breathes in unison. It is the appearance of the sacred and divine in each and every molecule. Every stone, rock, animal, person, breeze rain and boring afternoon is infused with sacred energy.

The Hanged Man cross is suggestive of a three-way crossroad. A choice is soon to be made. The halo around is head is a mark of divinity. His posture is a reversal of the World card. He reflects the beauty that is to come.

The Hanged Man can indicate a sacrifice but it is a worthy one. It is pausing for a moment, making room for possibility, and at the same time, using the space to look deeper at your present situation. He appears for you like a signpost on the road. He gives you a head's up that things are about to become wildly interesting.

The Hanged Man reflects the moment where the magician sees directly into "the source." It is the interconnection of all things in the unifying nature of energy and magic. Nothing ends. Energy never dies; it merely transforms. It describes the relationship between you and the universe. You and the universe are interconnected yet separate things (as above, so below). The Universe experiences itself through you. You are a Universe unto yourself. A piece of the divinity experiencing itself. The Hanged Man marks the moment you embody and understand this interconnection. It is the key to everything.

XIII. DEATH

Departure

"Out with the old and in with the new."

Key: Terminus, Carnage, Loss, Passage, Evolution.
Reversal: Paralysis, Solidifying.

Death is traditionally the most feared card in Tarot. The public takes the Death card at face value thinking it portends an actual end-of-life scenario. Beneath the surface, this card reflects the nature of change, generation, and evolution. Letting go offers the ability to anchor inside the present moment. Doing so allows you to act in accordance with true nature. To be fully alive, one must discard the past. This way you will not to be muddled down by it.

Death exists in the shadow areas of our psyche until we are forced to deal with it. Death is not the opposite of life. Death is the opposite of birth, a construct essential to enter the material world. Life itself is infinite. Death is the clearing space.

Death is marked as number thirteen. It is the uncanny number of strangeness and occult significance. Death is the energy keeping the material world fresh and new.

Death inhabits the shadows, forests, and thickets of gothic literature, film, and horror. Death is where we brush up against that which we cannot see or understand. How can we integrate Death's lessons? How can Death teach us how to live?

Esoterically, death occurs during the initiation into a magical or secret society. The old self drops away and gets replaced by a new reality. This is why a pair of towers in the distance contains a sun rising between them. The rising sun echoes the ascension of the spirit after transformational death. It is the awakening of the occult soul.

In this sense, the scene of this card is both death and resurrection. Four figures lay before Death reflecting the Court Card family and four elements. Only the child is unafraid. She is curious and does not back down or look away. The King's crown is tossed aside to signifying a new order. Fallen kings are common symbols on older versions of the Death card. A woman who looks like the Strength card turns her face to the side. A religious figure begs for mercy.

Death marches forward on his horse. The card appears to reflect fluidity and the forces of change. The Death card is the clearing of the path before you and an ascent to higher understanding. It is a new beginning that allows you to become free to possibility. When this card appears for you in a reading it has one important message: let go.

XIV. TEMPERANCE

Complexity

"Find equilibrium in change."

Key: Honing skills, Prudence, Synthesis, Administration, Complexity, Alchemy.
Reversed: Imbalance, Uneven.

Temperance is the angel who brings balance and fusion into your life. This card shows you how to energize opposing energies. It is how to merge and combine different ideas to arrive at fresh conclusions. It is also the card of balance and making sure you make room for everything in your life, most importantly, yourself. Temperance is the sacred and mundane, highs and lows, and every nuance in between.

The center and focal point of Temperance is the liquid she fuses. It is called Temperance, because, when we embody the card our consciousness tempers, combines and harmonizes our psychic and material natures. It is balancing the spiritual side of us along with the "real world" practical side. In a sense, she reflects a spiritual maturity and ability to balance between the seen and unseen as temper is used as a verb.

It is the energy of honing and getting better at what you do. It is returning repeatedly to the work and practices of your life, be they creative, spiritual, work related or a combination thereof. It is showing up and putting in the work, like tempering a sword to make it sharper.

Temperance and the Moon card mirror each other with pool and path. Temperance is day and the Moon is night. Temperance is your attention and activity while the Moon is your psyche and internal facilities.

The Temperance pond reflects the rich biodiversity of nature. It reminds us we are part of nature not separate from it. The pool of water is a symbol of new life and the subconscious. The angel is Gabriel. This is the messenger angel who acts as an intermediary between the sacred and profane or the invisible and visible worlds.

The distant path blazes up and into the mountains. This is the potential of where you might go. Divine light and brilliance await you. The circle upon the angel's head reflects solar power, the sun. The crown at the top of the mountains bears the occultist's secret of eternal life. It also reflects your crowning achievements when you apply lessons of Temperance in your life.

Above all, Temperance is the card of balance and complexity. It also displays the magic we make when we focus on what's in front of us and actively works with it, rather than be tempted by distraction. We stand inside shifting polarities at all time. How can we stay focused on those things that truly matter?

XV. DEVIL

Shadow

"Holding yourself hostage."

Key: Compulsion, Desecrate, Violence, Disaster, Hedonism.
Reversed: Triviality, Nonchalance.

The Devil reflects every part of you holding yourself hostage. It is repression, cruelty, and painful darkness. Satan is enduring archetype in literature, religion, and myth. The Devil has historically been a scapegoat whereby others are blamed for wrongdoings. "The Devil (booze, jazz, music, etc.) made me do it." Entire societies, as well as individuals have been used as scapegoats reaping disastrous consequence. The Devil is a convenient symbol that bears the projections of humanity that can't bear to take responsibility of their own actions.

The Devil can represent a base level of a disorder in the mind or psychic entropy. In this case it is mental illness but also anger, rage, jealousy. Envy and hatred sucking attention away from meaningful experiences. How do you deal with anger and control issues? How do you lash out at others?

The Devil and Magician share the exact same posture. The Magician channels while the Devil attempts maniacal control. The Magician's precise wand has become the Devil's flaming torch. Energy must flow. It cannot be forced or held tightly. Try to contain it and the damn will crack, the river will flood. Disaster ensues and unneeded suffering occurs.

The Devil card is abundant in your life when extreme control is exercised over any situation. It applies to all forms of abusive power from seeking intellectual or physical power over another to obsessive, compulsive cleaning. An individual either works in tandem with natural forces or faces dire consequences. The only thing we have control over is ourselves.

The Devil's wings are bat wings. Bats are traditionally agents of darkness. He is the archangel Uriel. His uplifted palm matches the Magician's hand and additionally evokes the Hierophant's sign of benediction also seen on the Ten of Swords. The symbol of Saturn, the planet of boundaries, embeds the Devil's palm. An inverted pentacle upon his forehead suggests the distortion of the natural world. The esoteric function of the Devil is laughter. Say what you must about the Devil but he always reflects a riotous good time (at least in the beginning he does). The Devil wants to indulge your every whim and fantasy. Whatever you desire, he wants you to have more of it; money, fame, sex, pleasure. But when is enough, enough?

The Devil card ultimately signifies illusion and control. It is abusive power and every role you play in it. He is your shadow self and all you repress inside of you. He is addiction, deception, and trickery. He is your immediate desires fulfilled at a dangerous cost. The only way to defeat this boss is to face him. Do you have the guts?

The Devil card is an inversion of the Lovers card. He infects the couple below with his power. Eleven grapes upon the female's tail reflect intoxication. The chains are symbolic of what is holding you hostage. Yet, the rusted neck chains are large enough to remove. Their hands are free. The power of escape is theirs yet they remain locked in his hellish dungeon. What are you allowing to control you? Are you willing to free yourself?

XVI. TOWER

Destruction
"Release of attachment."

Key: Agony, Tribulation, Ruin, Humbling, Unforeseen Disaster.
Reversed: Catastrophe but to a lesser degree.

The Tower card appears when you've danced with the Devil and lived to tell. The Devil has been greeted, defeated, and integrated. All false, inauthentic, and un-needed qualities disappear and fall into ruin. Everything changes, often in shock-ingly abrupt ways. Friendships shift. Jobs change. Circumstances completely dis-combobulate while they reform into a new normal. Different people are attracted to your light. Opportunities come knocking.

Tower moments feel jolting. It appears shocking to those around you as you make new and empowered decisions. Don't be surprised if there is a lack of support, surprise, or looks of wonder. Those who count will come around while the rest fall away.

The Tower is sometimes as drastic as a complete life makeover, a move, a new job, a complete hundred and eighty-degree turn. Other times, the Tower is a moment of crystal, clear clarity where there was once confusion. You are reborn in an ulti-mate "Aha!" moment.

Lightning strikes the great tower. Smoke and brimstone seep through that card as two figures fall to a merciless death. The rocky landscape reflects brilliant illumi-nation changing every known thing in the flash of an eye, demonstrates the power of thought, the genius of the mind. Immediate understanding radiates through the body and soul.

Yet, universal forces aren't finished. The lightning marks a moment of no return and unexpected upheaval. An energetic opening of epic proportion. Goosebumps erupt across the skin as life as you know life will never be the same. The Tower reflects the shattering quality of life as false pretenses are been destroyed by accep-tance of the Shadow as the occultist works her back up the Tree of Life.

The lightning in the card is representative of a spiritual force that wants to be made aware in this world. The zigzag shape of the lightning represents energy moving down the Tree of Life so it can appear in the physical world. In a sense, the Tower is the jolt that creates an opening and space for something new to arrive. That's why after all the pain and drama, the agony and the ecstasy, comes the Star.

Ultimately, the Tower is the destruction of what never fit to begin with. This is evident in the circular crown being knocked off a square tower. It is a needed re-calibration that organizes everything in a brand new way.

XVII. STAR

Peace

"Peace and quiet after the storm."

Key: Catharsis, Inspiration, Hope, Optimism, Clarity.
Reversed: Haughtiness, Arrogant.

The Star appears as the open, generous space, which comes to you after the Tower card's energy, destroys what is unneeded. The Star reflects an inspired space after a true energetic clearing. The Star is freedom in every way. It reminds you of what is possible when it is hard to see through the static. The Star is the soul opening. It is the card of possibility, life, and connection. It is the breeding ground of true magic.

Generosity fills the Star card with the ability to be kind to others and the self. Clarity illuminates you like helium in a balloon. The body is alive and open, warm, and receiving. This state of reception allows fresh ideas to burst forth. An unexpected possibility, a thrilling opportunity, a situation beyond your wildest dreams, is now available.

The Star is naked, losing all self-consciousness. It reflects the ultimate vulnerability. She is peaceful yet active. Celestial radiance showers upon her. This is the energy of artistry and muse. It reflects your connection to water, earth, and sky. She operates freely. The Devil has relinquished his grip. The Tower cleared the decks. Hope, relief, and pleasure surround you.

The loss of self-consciousness permeates the Star card. Children are naturally unaware of how they appear to others. They have not yet learned to be fearful. The release of self-consciousness occurs as trust is rebuilt in yourself. Self-consciousness consumes innate psychic energy. We think of how we look, act or are being judged by others. The ego stands at the fore. The Star releases us from those bonds allowing us to merge with cosmic unity.

Starlight is divine light but we can engage in it directly. Look to a star in the night sky and the star looks back at us. It is the essence of muse and artist. Inspiration from above infusing the body with purpose. The Devil and Tower rattled us to our core. The Star serves to soothe like the calm clarity setting over a field after a thunderstorm has passed. The Star foreshadows the innocence of the child seen in the Sun.

This card appears to mark emotional clearings and inspiration. New realities are enjoyed. Deep and true motivation occurs. Sacred space is cleared. Hope springs once again and life rejuvenates itself.

XVIII. MOON

Mystery
"Emergence of latent possibility."

Key: Mystery, Occult, Hidden Adversaries, Beguilement, Obscurity.
Reversed: Error and Deception of Lesser Impact.

Expect wild and uncanny things to unfold when the Moon card appears for you in a reading. The Moon is the card of myth and monster. It is reality and landscape altered. Dreamlike visions pass through the imagination of sleepers, artists, and seekers. Dark prophecies are uttered. Spells cast. Devils dance at the crossroads. Intense psychic energy and the binding nature of intuition, at first placid and peaceful in the High Priestess, is now electric, undeniable, and permeating everything.

The Moon card reflects an instinct, idea and form rising in your subconscious. It wants to take shape in the world but you must allow it to rise. This new urge is so strange and unknown you require gentle moonlight to coax it out. It gives you space to encounter the emergence of something new in a safe space. Moonlight softens all edges.

The Moon lets us know our situation is in flux. Lunar cycles echo the transitory nature of human life, female menstrual cycles, and nature of all things. No emotion, life cycle, or horrific circumstance last forever. Good, bad, indifferent, life's nature, the psyche's nature – ebbs and flows, hustles and flows, like ocean tides. "Yes," the Moon says, "Things get weird, scary even. The unknown is terrifying. Unimaginable things occur. But not forever. Nothing is forever."

The Moon card's rich symbolism includes a crayfish moving from the liquid of the unconscious. This crustacean is your instinct. The path between the towers is your imagination's journey into the unknown. The dog (left) and wolf (right) are fears present in the natural mind. The dog, wolf, and crayfish also symbolize the base animal nature of the unthinking and non-analytical mind. It is the place where the imagination takes flight. The two glowing towers are the left and right side of the Tree of Life. The path is the integrated center. The pool reflects subconscious depths. The pool is a symbolic device of what is within us giving shape to fear. The Moon and the Sun's image are graphically combined to demonstrate the moonlight as a reflection of the Sun. It reminds us that life in this world is a reflection of the divine. Our path, our journey is best navigated through our intuition.

Explore the path appearing before you, no matter how odd it might appear. Strange turns, uncanny moments, and moonlight transform familiar things into something new. Use weirdness and unfamiliarity as opportunities to reexamine current beliefs. The sun will rise. When it does, you'll have seen more than you ever imagined.

XIX. SUN

Creator

"Manifestation is the natural state of the universe."

Key: Prosperity, Contentment, Material Abundance, Success, Vitality.
Reversed: Same meaning, less intense.

The Sun card appears to reflect radiant health, blossoming manifestation, and expansion of all qualities in life. It is the heat of pleasure, long summer days, and winking sunflowers. It is the engine making all life possible. The peaceful face of the sun evokes kind advice as if to say no matter what happens, you'll be okay.

Your heart's desire expands and grows larger. This card reveals the unfolding of who you are. It's what you are capable of as you take active steps to move forward. It is you in your glory riding into freedom.

Happiness and joy are yours. The sun is spiritual consciousness. It is the place in which the soul becomes aware of itself within the integration of divine light. Symbolically, the child on the horse is the Fool reborn. This connection is made by the red feather on his head. The Sun watches over the Fool card at the beginning of the deck. It rises in symbolic resurrection in the Death card (who also wears a red feather). Now the Sun takes center stage and everything that was once hinted potential is expanding forth.

The sunflowers represent solar energy. It is standing at attention, holding your power, and facing the future with clarity and purpose. The garden wall reflects a boundary that is crossed. What was once nurtured and protected can now proceed out and into the unknown. It marks the moments you cross into the unknown with complete ease and assurance.

You as the Sun's child – it knows exactly what it is you're doing, where you are going and what your intentions are. The child's lack of clothing denotes a willingness to be vulnerable. It is also innocence. Children are not born with shame but taught to shame themselves. There is no reason to hide who you truly are.

In a way, the Sun card reflects your journey home to yourself. You accept yourself and the world complies. There is inherent freedom and pleasure. The child's banner, also a flame, reflects a nurturing energy with the strength to last a lifetime. This card also reflects gardening and house and home. It is the metaphorical and physical restoration of who you are in every aspect.

XX. JUDGEMENT

Evolution

"A wake-up call."

Key: Revolutionary Change, Regeneration, Results, Awaken, Release.
Reversed: Dastardly, Weak.

Judgement brings you to the point of no return. Nothing will ever be the same. You see what you are capable of and more importantly you no longer ignore it. Choice evaporates as you find the direct line to your eventuality. Others take note. Ramifications are everywhere. There is no going back. The train leaves the station. The airplane's aloft. The transformation is nearly complete. You embrace your true destiny.

Change permeates beneath the surface of everything in life. These moments are felt in small ways. Your clothes and home don't feel right. Things that used to comfort and give you pleasure feel hollow as new interests take shape. Extroverts stay home. Introverts hit the town. New boundaries, walls, and encasements are formed. Doors open, possibility comes knocking, intuition flows freely.

Archangel Michael, the angel of protection. He sounds his trumpet to the figures below. The trumpet's song is a true calling, a wake-up sign, the right lyric heard at the right time. Where is the calling inside yourself? Do art, nature, and poetry call to you? What is your siren song? What is beautiful enough that it can't be ignored? How does your "lower nature" or the material, earthly bound self hear your true calling?

The dead rise from their coffins. The figure's nudity expresses vulnerability. The children reflect innocence. Families represent unity. The mother, father, and child's upward facing and open arms suggest a welcome embrace of invitation.

The entire card is symbolic of the Last Judgement in the biblical sense. It can be read using all of those metaphors and allegories. The Last Judgement has been painted the world over by artists, from Michelangelo to William Blake to dozens of films and works of literature. Judgement's iconic use, whether comical, serious or biblical, always marks the ending on the known world.

Justice represents the entire earth rising to the call of truth, "as above, so below." You are the world and the world is you. You bring the earthly world with you as you rise to embrace the call of your heart. You transform not only yourself but also everything along with you.

XXI. WORLD

Integration

"Everything in its place."

THE WORLD.

Key: Pure pleasure, Success Defined, Journey, Euphoria, Travel, Perfection.
Reversed: Idle, Sluggish.

You, as the World dancer, move in a state of sheer perfection. What was intimated by the Wheel of Fortune as the nature of the universe is now embodied inside your skin and bones, in your actions and gestures, your thoughts and feelings. Opposing qualities are integrated. Self-consciousness is cast aside. Complete trust is formed. You are the dazzling essence. Your talents, qualities, sensitivities infuse every action.

A glorious moment of completion. Beauty and brilliance are profound, like the possibility is birthed in the Fool. It is fresh and brimming with possibility. Your pattern is forever altered. Salvation occurs. You are the universe and the most creative and magical act you will ever partake in. The ego dissolves. Deep time is experienced. Time vanishes.

The World holds two magic wands in opposition to the Magician who held a single wand. Her wands reverberate as a constant source of power. Rather than direct the energy, like the Magician, she embodies circuitous motion.

Four corner figures are a Tetramorph, a biblical reference to the first chapter of Ezekiel reflecting a man, lion, ox and eagle. The four creatures represent the four corners/directions: north, south, east and west and the four suits of Tarot: Wands, Cups, Swords and Pentacles. Her green wreath is oval shaped in the shape of a zero, the number of the Fool who rises to meet her. The oval also suggests the birth canal through which new life enters the world.

The World is the ultimate card. It is the end of the Major Arcana. It is the Big Bang. Perfected and complete. It is the sweet spot of life when all energies mingle, inside and outside, meeting in a raptured, ecstatic union. Your desire is met. You share your gifts with the world. You hold nothing back. You are fully alive and present. You have ever desired. It is the ultimate state of bliss.

Travel, excitement and movement surround you as you go with the flow. Lost in the moment, time ceases to concern you. Complete integration with the world around you. Effortless ease replaces stress. Freedom of the self reigns. This card is you in all your glory. You as you were always meant to be, success and infinity. It represents your ultimate victory.

CHAPTER FOUR

THE MINOR ARCANA

MINORS

Minors represent forces that are more ordinary in the Querent's life. They do not relate directly to the fundamentals cogs of the Universe or of the Querent's life, but rather concur to build all kinds of everyday and human experiences. They are not less important of the Majors, but they are definitely more approachable and down to earth.

Compared to the Majors, the Minors do not have an archetypal name, because they do not refer to any specific archetype. The number (or rank, in case of the Court Cards) and Suit, however, can be very useful to complete the understanding and interpretation of any Minor.

ACE OF CUPS

"Emotional outpouring."

Key: Overflowing emotion, Heart canter, Bliss, Comfort, Elation, Exuberance.
Reversed: False Heart, Deviant.

The Ace of Cups is the joy of your heart bursting with happiness. It appears when you feel safe and connected enough to share your feelings with whomever you come into contact with. It signifies creative flow and the ability to pour everything you feel into the task at hand. It is using the emotional intelligence of the heart, which is the ability to move from compassion. Compassion and love is everflowing which is why five streams pour into the waters below.

The Ace of Cups is being so vulnerable that no instinct, idea, or feeling is repressed. It is the release of everything you feel and the beauty indicative of speaking from the heart. It is having love for yourself and others. It is sharing all qualities of emotion and moving with the flow. It is the cleansing energy of fresh water such like a shower, waterfall, or even a good cry.

The card reflects abundance and having more than you will ever need. This security provides you with the ability to share your thoughts, feeling, and ideas with others. It is infectious, buoyant energy.

The rejuvenation of the Ace of Cups appears like a baptismal font. The waters wash us physically and metaphorically. The card evokes the auditory sound of bubbling, cascading water. The Ace of Cups is a heart opener and linked to the heart chakra. It is a healed and healthy heart.

The Cup receives the dove's gift while the waters pour forth. The image leans into Christian symbolism with a dove and wafer appearing on the card. The dove reflects peace and purity while the wafer reflects divinity. The ability to both give and receive.

The water beneath the Ace of Cups is dotted with lotus flowers and water lilies. Lotus is a symbol of rebirth, resurrection, and creation. It roots deeply into murky mud, closes at nightfall, and blooms as the sun rises across the morning sky.

All Aces are the seeds of their suit, holding all the qualities yet to be expressed. The Ace of Cups contains every imaginable emotion, from high to low, from melancholia to jubilation. This is why Aces hold endless potential and always mark the beginning of a new cycle.

TWO OF CUPS

"Greeting the heart's desire."

Key: True Love, Tenderness, Affinity, Adoration, Marriage.
Reversed: Keeping personal happiness at bay for an odd, ill-fitting reason.

The Two of Cups is your heart's desire reflected back to you. It is that magical moment of finding your other half. It is like-mindedness and genuine compatibility as found in dearest, closest friends, and most romantic of relationships. It is meeting someone new and feeling like you have known them forever. It is also those friends who you don't see for years and once together it's as if no time has passed. You pick up right where you left off.

This card also signifies marriage and pleasure. A Caduceus, a winged rod with two snakes reflects negotiation and balance. The red lion reflects the element of air. The symbol is often connected to the messenger god Mercury. Be on the lookout for messages regarding social engagements, friends, and love.

The structure of the card is strikingly similar to the Lovers. Two figures create a graphic triangle with a higher being floating above them. The landscape behind them rises at the midpoint as the mountain does in the Lovers card.

Just as the male's gaze on the Lovers card looks upon the female, so does the male in the Two of Cups reach towards the female in a gesture of approach and invitation. Someone is asking you to join them. Who is it? What desires you? Will you accept their offer?

Both figures are clothed as if in an Elizabethan wedding. The male dressed in red and yellow symbolizing fire (a masculine element associated with Wands) while the female dons blue, white, and green the colors of Water (a feminine elemental associated with Cups). The female wears a laurel wreath, an interlocking set of bay leaves representing victory.

Occult books have described the card as the "harmony of masculine and feminine united." As such, we see the binary nature of the self and the balance of relationships. Each half of the card mirrors the other and it sometimes appears to show that we are only showing another person what we think they want to see.

THREE OF CUPS

"Delight in camaraderie."

Key: Accomplishment, Healing, Relief, Friendship.
Reversed: Excess physical pleasure and overwhelming sensory delight.

The Three of Cups reflects the abundant joy of friendship, sharing and celebration. This is love and community, a gathering to celebrate friendship. It is lifting one another up, making toasts, and general revelry if not a pleasure-filled indulgence. This card reflects a strong sense of belonging and purpose in one's life. It is feeling like part of a larger community. Self-confidence and an excellent sense of self worth are at an all time high.

Work and toil reach a conclusion as indicated by the lush field bursting with the bounty of fall harvest. The euphoric bacchanalian element of cups overflowing potential for loss of inhibition. This is reflected in the grapes held by the young maiden on the right of the card (a secret link to the Nine of Pentacles where a female stands inside a vineyard). The grapes also link to the Devil card where grapes are found on the female's tail. This is a reminder of the dark side of drinking and merriment and when such bountiful occasions became daily habits.

The crown of flowers invokes fertility festivals, youthful adore, and vitality. The three cups make a perfect triangle reminding us of the creative nature of the number three. Laughter is the medicine of the soul and also an energetic opening.

A darker read of this card reveals Macbeth's three witches dancing in glee over the success of their spells while others prefer to see happiness and pleasure. At its worst, this card reflects being left out of a social gathering and feeling like an outsider where you were once welcomed. Thankfully, the Three of Cups usually marks a happy occasion where pleasure is shared.

FOUR OF CUPS

"Can you see opportunity before you?"

Key: Apathy, Reluctance, Fatigue, Imagined Problems.
Reversed: Omen, Prophecy.

The Four of Cups appears in reading to reveal an unseen opportunity. Something is offered to you, can you see what it is? Look up and around you. What you seek is right there. It might be the magic elixir you've been searching for.

Fours imply stability and thus this card reflects stable emotions in functioning support. You are ready to face whatever is being offered. Bring what is interesting and fascinating into your awareness. Don't just sit and wait to be served with genius, actively cultivate it.

Four of Cups symbolism aligns with Buddhist principles because the figure sits beneath the tree, like Buddha under the boddhi tree. Buddha's Sanskrit name means, "awakened one." Take a cue from eastern philosophy by remembering that meditation encourages emotional balance. It reminds you of fleeting feelings that will soon become something else. The emotions represented by Cups, especially darker emotions like hatred, resentment, and anger, are often the source of great pain. Learn to let emotions pass without reacting out of them.

We recall our connection to nature and the rejuvenating power of the natural world when looking at the tree of the Four of Cups. Three cups stand at the front of the card to remind you of experience and manifestation of the past. Trust your internal knowing.

This card cautions against complacency. Bring your whole self to what you choose to engage in. If you don't take advantage of opportunities they will become less available. Stay engaged within your network of friends and colleagues. Be willing to take risks, share ideas, and offer opinions.

The Four of Cups darkest nature can be understood as disconnection. World-weariness is the bridge to disillusionment. Rest, nurture, and regain the balance of the emotions. Accept help from others. Know that nothing lasts forever.

FIVE OF CUPS

"Inheritance but not what was expected"

Key: Sadness and depression, Troubled Marriage, Addiction.
Reversed: Relations, Ancestry.

The Five if Cups is a dark, sometimes, deviant card. Modern readers often call this the card of addiction. It is important to remember how addiction manifests in multiple forms. We may be addicted to thought patterns, people, and ways of life as well as to drugs, nicotine, or booze. The three spilled cups to the left side reflect what has been consumed and lost. This is the price we have already paid. Poison remains in the two remaining upright cups. Will you turn to ingest more or will you move across the bridge to find salvation on the other side? Ask yourself, what price you pay for indulgence?

The figure's dark cloak reflects depression. The number five often brings challenges that are to be overcome. There is a lack of joy and desire to hide from the world. Could the figure be crying into his cups? Has he kicked the cups because what was once a comfort has turned to poison?

The card often represents emotional qualities we have inherited from our family via genetics and/or conditioning. No matter where our emotional makeup is cultivated, it is important to stay true to who you are. The two standing cups show you that you can choose your reaction to any feeling or situation.

The figure's stance inside the cups is being too close to the emotions of a situation. The need to remove oneself, to gain distance by crossing over the bridge and reassessing the situation from a new vantage point offers numerous options. Walk away.

Should the card appear to mark a certain moment of melancholia or sorrow, the cups serve an important reminder. Feel your feelings, do not repress them. Do not linger too long in sadness. Release attachments to what has vanished. Do not be fooled by retrospect and trapped inside of time. Once imprisoned by thoughts of what was or could have been, you might miss extraordinary happiness looking you right in the face. Become available to all the good things you desire.

A reversed Five of Cups often appears to show you have moved past old addictions. Issues once rattling you to the core are vanquished. It is the resiliency of the human spirit.

SIX OF CUPS

"You can go home again."

Key: Glimmers of the past, Walk down memory lane,
Past affections, New realizations.
Reversed: What Comes Around Goes Around, Renewal.

The Six of Cups is often noted as the card of nostalgia and a walk down memory lane. From the darkness and despair reflected in the Five of Cups, hope is reborn and sunshine blooms anew. The card reflects gifts from the heart as an older boy passes a flowering cup to a younger girl. The figure's heads are covered by hood and veil suggesting protection. The cups are bursting with flowers implying an important relationship manifesting real results. Indeed, something rich and sustaining occurs.

A figure, perhaps a soldier, is walking away in the background. It marks an authority figure disappearing. It leaves the children to enjoy their own magical world. We can also understand this action as you being willing to walk away from the qualities, people, and haunting memories no longer serving you.

The card takes place within the courtyard of a medieval town. It denotes a safe, soft space as the walls are meant to keep danger at bay. It reminds you to allow yourself an opportunity to revisit the past in pleasant ways. We can return to certain moments with the wisdom of experience and thus come to understand events of the past in a richer more nuanced way.

The Tarot can act as a mirror of memory. Just as a mirror will never show you exactly what you look like, so does our perception play tricks on events and occurrences. We can only truly know how we felt. Scent, sight, and taste will often transport us like a time machine back to a specific moment of memory.

The Six of Cups appears to remind you to accept new friends who will someday be called your old friends. Open your heart and give of yourself freely. Be willing to accept gifts when they are offered. Engage in delightful visions of the past. Reach out to the people who have meant the most to you. Let them know how you feel.

SEVEN OF CUPS

"Everything that could be."

Key: Imagination, Possibilities, Reflection, Gifts, Visions.
Reversed: Boldness, Decision.

The Seven of Cups reflects visions of what is possible. It is conjuring dreams before you. Cups appear as delightful new choices. Sparkly delights await. Possibility beguiles the senses. You've paid, played, and now you've won the carnival game. Time to choose your prize. Keep eyes wide open and perceptions clear.

Wonderment and fantasy surround you. The floating images in the air might be a personal projection. In that case, the cups reflect facets of imagination, each with its own unique treasure. We can only focus on one thing at a time. Which do you select? Move from your gut. The body knows before the head.

What if the cups appear as a trick or puzzle? What if you select the wrong cup and like Indiana Jones, a boulder comes barreling toward you? There is always a chance you will be crushed. Remember that not choosing is also a choice.

In some cases the Seven of Cups appears to mark glowing creativity. It could be supernatural visions such as Joan of Arc was prone to having. It will also mark clairvoyance, which is the talent or ability to see past, present and future events before they have happened.

The secret of the Seven of Cups is that each cup connects to a Major Arcana card. Beginning from the top left and moving right:

Cup #1 – The female head corresponds to the Empress and Venus (recall the sign of Venus on the Empress's garments).

Cup #2 – The veiled figure is the High Priestess and the Moon (recall the High Priestess's Moon crown).

Cup #3 – The snake is the Magician and Mercury (recall the Magician's snake belt which devours itself around the Magician's waist).

Lower left and moving right:

Cup #4 – The castle on the high rocks is the Tower card (recall how the Tower sits upon a mountain peak).

Cup #5 – Glittering jewels are the Wheel of Fortune (recall the Wheel represents fate, fortune, and destiny).

Cup #6 – The wreath is the World Card (recall the World card's wreath). The skull is the illusion of success and its deceptive qualities.

Cup #7 – The crouching dragon is the Sun (Sun energy is fiery like dragon breath).

EIGHT OF CUPS

"Walking away from what has been."

Key: Departure, Movement, Transition, Journey, Release, Onward.
Reversed: Feasting, Celebration.

The Eight of Cups reflects a particular moment when you have the choice to stay exactly where you are but you risk everything by leaving it behind. It must be done. Departure is imminent. Explore new heights. In many ways, this card can be understood as the Hermit at the beginning of his journey up the mountain. Sometimes, you have to walk away from what you have in order to get what you want.

The metaphor of taking the "high road" reflects the choice to not engage with the messy emotions of others (symbolized by the cups). Do not become entangled with issues that were never yours to begin with. Stay true to yourself. It is your time to journey.

A curious and palpable magic dances across still water. A rare solar eclipse occurs as the moon passes over the sun and casts its shadowy dimness upon the earth below. Anything could happen. It probably will.

It appears to some that the graphic nature of the card depicts a ninth cup who has become a figure of the person walking away. In this sense, we can understand the card as suggesting the beginning of an adventure you have always imagined becoming real. What you've seen in the mind's eye is now unfolding.

There are many journey cards in the deck; however, the Eight of Cups speaks of a journey undertaken alone. It is the road only you can travel. In this sense, the Eight of Cups is the call to the greatest adventure of your life. Pack your bags, make your plans, but cast them aside as soon as you depart. The wandering passport is yours to do with as you please. Let your dreams be your guidebook. Abandon your itinerary. Leave supplies behind you. Where you are going requires but one thing: you.

NINE OF CUPS

"Your wish will come true!"

Key: Fulfillment of dreams, Advantage, Satisfaction, Your wish will come true.
Reversed: Liberation, Truth.

The Nine of Cups appears to let you know your wish will come true! Nine is the ever-lucky number of fulfillment. The card represents complete pleasure and ultimate happiness. The cups look like trophies and awards lined up in your name. Allow yourself to bask in recognition. This card signifies you as an object of success and affection. You have worked hard. Enjoy the efforts you have made. Linger in your happy place for as long as you can. Agree to your own enjoyment of life.

This hidden nature of the Nine of Cups reminds us, "Be careful what you wish for." There may be consequences you never imagined. This might also mean that we don't always get what we want but we get what we need.

The figure on the card appears like a genie granting your intention. Genies have a rich deep history that moves far beyond simple wish-granting skills. Genies in the Middle East are rooted in Mesopotamian myth and legend. They are often demon and fairy like creatures that can possess another person and cause great disturbances, distress, addiction, and even death. We can remember this in the context of what we are willing to do to others and ourselves in order to get what we want.

Conjure pleasure as often as you can. One need not cast complicated magic in order to bring about satisfaction, although such activities contain their own sacred joy. Examine the Eight, Nine and Ten of Cups together. It suggests a familiar narrative and echoes a popular and moralistic sentiment; take a risk (Eight of Cups), good things will come (Nine of Cups) and you'll live happily ever after (Ten of Cups).

TEN OF CUPS

"Happily ever after."

Key: Delightful environment, Home life, Friendship, Family, Satisfaction.
Reversed: Darkness, Violence.

The Ten of Cups appears like the finale of a play. Loose ends are tied up, villains vanquished, and a happy ending ensues. It is the maturity of family and romantic relationships. Frolicking children, fierce companionship, and a happy home life. It is the end of a story, chapter, and cycle.

The nuclear family is representative of any type of home life and the energy therein. It can show us happiness in the workplace, on vacation, or in an actual home where peace and generosity reign.

This is the only card in the deck holding all four court card family positions; King: father, Queen: mother, Knight: boy, Page: girl. The male figures wear red signifying the quality of fire or wands. The females wear blue to signify the aquatic nature of creativity and dreams. Energy and vitality is balanced by imagination and emotion.

The rainbow reminds us that the storms have past. The joy on display has been fought for. This simple fact reminds us not to take other's happiness for granted. Things don't always look like they appear. We never know what individuals, couples and families have been through, even when things look bright and shiny on the outside. The couple embraces, welcomes the rainbow. It is nature's signal that the zeitgeist is over. Thunder and rain retreat into the distance.

Strong emotional health thrives inside the Ten of Cups. Peace, generosity, and compassion are important to cultivate but they also feel good. The children can reflect anyone in your life who you care for and watch over.

Tens reflect the end of a cycle. As the suit of cups reaches its conclusion it is useful to consider opening a new chapter. Enjoy what lay around you and cherish people who bring you joy.

PAGE OF CUPS

"A highly psychic and creative youth."

Key: News, Messages, Psychic Ability, Contemplative Youth.
Reversed: Sneaky, Savvy.

The Page of Cups represents the attitude of a playful and open-minded nature. No barriers exist inside the boundless qualities of youthful joy and curiosity. Do you remember playing imagination games as a child? When was the last time you allowed your imagination to run free? Intuitive insights occur with frequency when you stay open to possibility. Pay attention to your daydreams. Follow them where they lead to discover yourself in a new and curious place.

The Page of Cups signifies wild creativity and a personality unafraid to express their feelings. The creative capacity of Page of Cups types suggests you will often find them inside art and music studios. They are well suited towards any type of creative work employing their fertile imagination and intrinsic talents. They are the lovers and creators of expression of all sorts.

A fish pops out of the cup to reflect visionary qualities. Waite explains it is "pictures of the mind taking form." The page wears a 15th century style of English clothing denoting wealth. Lotus flowers, the Golden Dawn's symbol for the element of water, dot the tunic. Gentle waters are painted upon the scrim behind the page. It suggests a calm approach and peaceful surroundings to aid pleasant meanderings of the mind.

The card suggests adopting an open attitude toward all challenges. Employ curiousness about the world around you. Page of Cups types are prone to psychic flashes, deep intuitive connection, and empathy towards others. They are likely to see ghosts and detect the subtle energies surrounding them. They are likely to sleep walk, experience night terrors, and have out of body experiences. Pat attention to how emotions affect your physical body. The Page of Cups holds deep soul truth like a young High Priestess. Meditation is suggested for the busy mind. Connect with your younger self through pleasurable, familiar activities.

KNIGHT OF CUPS

"Dreamy and poetic suitor."

Key: Appearance, Advance, Invitation, Presence, Enticement.
Reversed: Swindle, Sham.

The Knight of Cups oozes love, romance, and sweet nothings. He is an epic lover who uses every resource at his fingertips to seduce you. He'll use words, gifts, and surprises to tell you how special you are. He takes his time and means everything he says. This is the suitor who sings your praises and anticipates your needs. He can sometimes appear duplicitous and as vapid as mist because he feels so deeply about everything. His feelings often extend to other people. He doesn't do this to be cruel it is just in his nature to find poetry in everything.

The Knight of Cups appears in a spread to let you know a message or invitation is on the way. Arrival is imminent. High praise will help you advance toward your objective. Remember you can always collect more flies with honey. Approach others in a kind and loving manner. There's no need to be false in this. Find something appealing about everyone you interact with in order to romance and charm them. Use words and gestures carefully to make others feel special.

The Knight of Cups is a deep and emotional lover with the sensitivity of a poet and artist. The Knight of Cups is a dreamy fellow who's horse carries a slow and steady energy. The wings of Hermes, the messenger god, appear on his helmet and heels. Fish are embroidered into his tunic and are emblematic of the suit of Cups, the element of water, and the zodiacal sign of Pisces. The landscape is dry sand and rock quenched by a blue river. The meandering water quenches an acrid, thirsty landscape. A dreamlike quality fills the card. It is a reminder of the wondrous places romance will carry you off to.

QUEEN OF CUPS

"Leading with your heart forward."

Key: Vulnerable strength empowering others, Empath, Dreamer, Prophetic, Seer, Devotion.
Reversed: Emotionally empty, Lost in imagination and fantasy.

The Queen of Cups is the most empathetic card in the deck. She is the therapist, caregiver, and Tarot reader due to her ability to look deep into the soul of another person and "see" them. She carries the ocean's depths of understanding. Her compassionate nature is due to the fact that she's experienced ups and downs, highs and lows herself. She recognizes herself in others when she sees people delighted, dour and every emotion in between.

She's the perfect Tarot reader because of her ability to see through the bottom of the situation. She is able to cross thresholds of the imagination, enter worlds of archetype, and receive angelic messages. It is always saying the very words a person needs to hear and backing it up with a genuine desire for them to be satiated and seen.

Queen of Cups qualities appear in other people who are extremely sensitive. They tend to love animals. They are equally comfortable as the artist or the muse and are often switching roles. She is the intuitive and psychic soul who has honed her gifts to share with the world. She delights herself with her artistic and intuitive gifts.

The darker side of the Queen of Cups is seen when giving over too much of herself to others. She may confuse the line between herself and another person, especially who's who are suffering. Drawn to close to pain and struggle, she may take these qualities on as her own. Therefore, it is important for you have the self-knowledge and control, recognize, and respect your own boundaries.

The Queen of Cups is drawn at the sea in front of the White Cliffs of Dover. She gazes at a Cup as if it's a dreamlike vision before her. Cherub mermaids decorate her throne and the engraved clam shell behind the Queen's head. Each clam shell is the symbol of her zodiacal assignment, Cancer. Her dress merges into the water, colored blue and green, like the waters surrounding her. It is as if she is an apparition dreamed of the ocean itself, a ghostly vision that welcomes all. She is love and devotion to all.

KING OF CUPS

"If you can dream it, you can do it."

Key: Arts and sciences, Creative intelligence, Fairness.
Reversed: Rogue, Double-dealer.

The King of Cups sees the world in terms of what is possible. He is a wise advisor and confidant whose glass is always full. Both the King and Queen of Cups harbor the ability to navigate the ocean's depths and dangers above. This includes understanding their own emotional state and the fluidity of other people's emotions and artistry.

The King of Cups is guided by his instincts and emotions yet not controlled or manipulated by them. He is often found working in the spotlight for the public good. Listening and interacting with this type of personality always surprises you. You walk away having learned a new way to look at any situation or how to understand another person. The King of Cups offers new lenses with which to understand the world. This is why he excels at arts and science.

The King of Cups appears in others when you see people who are able to bring their creative projects to fruition, no matter what obstacles stand in their way. It is a sheer dedication to a vision. It is belief in the self that overrides seemingly insurmountable obstacles. He is the artist, the film director, the philosopher.

The dark side of the King of Cups appears in people prone to emotional outbursts and extreme highs and lows. The personality whose entire ego is wrapped up in the success or failure of their current projects. This energy is exhaustive to be around. A reversed King of Cups is also evident in people with extreme creative blockage.

The fish pendant around the King's neck as well as the ocean and sea creatures are visual clues connecting him to the element of water. The King even wears scaly fish footwear. The high seas and waves upon represent his ability to go with the flow. The water is his imagination, ever teeming with life and possibility. The fish monster to his left side is a symbol of a love of myth and ability to skirt danger. The tall ship is a symbolic of stories and visions that transport others. His entire self is in love with adventure, entertainment, and risk.

ACE OF PENTACLES

"Opportunity presents itself."

Key: Riches, Merriment, Ideal Happiness, Euphoria, Manifestation.
Reversed: Downside of great wealth.

Opportunity abounds in the Ace of Pentacles. An offering, perhaps unexpected, marks the beginning on a new path. There is tremendous potential for growth appearing in real world results. It is a building block in the areas of finance, health, and the physical world.

The surrounding garden is a reminder of what has already blossomed and tells you what is possible. A garden gate, festooned with ivy and flowers, shows you a door of opportunity is opening. The path entices you to walk out of this proverbial garden of comfort zones to seek wild, new adventures. Distant mountains remind you of the heights it is possible to ascend.

A close inspection marks the miracle of physical manifestation in the material realm as symbolized by a five-pointed star inside a double circle, the symbol of a Pentagram. This symbol dates back to ancient Mesopotamia. The circle is the basic building block of life, the shape of our planets and stars as well as molecules and the cells within our body. It contains the power and energy of the sun and life giving essence. This vibrancy is what makes all things blossom and grow. It moves with adherence to natural rhythms and changing seasons. What wants to blossom inside of you? Will you stand in the shade or allow the sun's energy to infuse you?

The golden color of the pentacle connects to alchemical gold. Vibrate your financial energy by saving and spending well. Indulge in the physical world and sensory pleasure. Give gifts often. You are the best gift you can give to the world.

Stay open and ready to receive in daily life by giving of yourself. Pay it forward. Many of us are taught that it is better to give than receive however the joy of receiving offers an opportunity for connection and intimacy.

TWO OF PENTACLES

"A pleasant choice is a hand."

Key: Duality, Recreation, Delight, A delicate dance.
Reversed: Pretending to have fun.

The Two of Pentacles appears to reflect duality and choice. Options have appeared and the final decision is in your hands. Either option is good; it is just a matter of personal preference. You can have fun with what's surrounding you. Unintended consequences change your initial plans but you are well suited to go with the flow.

The lemniscate, a sideways eight, is the symbol of infinity. Arthur Waite called it the "endless cord." It surrounds the pentacles and is a deep reminder to go with the flow and not push too hard in any direction. The figure is on a stage, dancing a jig. It reminds you to be light-footed. The situation does not require a heavy hand. Apply your lightest touch and stay open to inspiration. The waves on the scrim behind the figure reflect the changing nature of your situation. There are many more things to come and the energy is fluid. Stay lightly focused on your task, especially if it is pleasant. Enjoy the process. There's no need to over think. Simply, pay attention.

The Two of Pentacles mirrors the Magician card who in earlier, historical decks, portrayed a juggler. Both cards contain a lemniscate and each bear the posture of moving energy from above to below. The Magician's results are seen in the Two of Pentacles which is the practical every day world.

The background ships portent further evolution. They suggest elements of travel and the hands of fate who summon unseen storms and squalls over those who sail the lightly on the seas. Step lightly; yet look out for what's coming down the road. Lastly, this card is a performance. It begs the questions, who are you performing for right now? Are you dancing to the beat of someone else's drum, or your own?

THREE OF PENTACLES

"Creative collaboration across professional fields."

Key: Industry, Trade, Aristocracy, High Society, Patrons.
Reversed: Taking the easy route.

The Three of Pentacles appears to remind us of the value of collaborating with others. Especially when are creating something. Now is the time for physical or metaphorical renovation. It pays off to bring in experts to help you. They could be technical, financial, emotional or creative support.

This card reflects the nature of progression and building blocks. The three figures are placed within an ancient monastery or stone chapel. A monk looks up at the workman. The workman is a Freemason. His Masonic symbols are a bench, apron, and tool. The ancient lineage of this card connects to myth, legend, and the mystery of existence. Although you may be concerned with material things like money, completion of a project, and success, there are far deeper implications grounding the work that you do. This connects it to the fabric of reality. It suggests lineage, even nobility.

The triangle of pentacles set in stone above the figures is indicative of the creative principal of three. It is the shape of divinity as evoked across cultures from the Father, Son, Holy Ghost to the Maiden, Mother, and Crone. This is a reminder that whatever we build in the material world has roots in the unseen and invisible. That all forms of manifestation spring from the intelligence that wanted it to come into creation. We may think we are the ones with the master plan but a greater energy and force is moving through us. Are we dreaming or is the dream dreaming us? When the Three of Pentacles appears in a reading it is a reminder to get back to work.

FOUR OF PENTACLES

"Identifying with material possessions."

Key: Grasping at resources, Inheriting money, Stability, Gifts.
Reversed: Uncertainty, Tension.

The Four of Pentacles shows up to tell you have what you need. The city behind the figure is what he has already built. Hard work and clever planning paid off but do not become attached to what is ephemeral.

The card often appears to reflect miserly tendencies. The figure is desperately grasping to his financial resources. The pull of the material world has proven irresistible. What are you clinging to? You may hold it so fiercely that you wind up destroying it.

The figure wears a crown signifying early success. He is yet to be crowned king. Fours are the stable building block numbers. You have a solid foundation upon which you can build anything you like. Do not fear your early success. You will not lose what you have gained. It is more than you think.

The pentacle over his head aligns with the crown chakra, which connects us to our highest thoughts and inspiration. It reminds us that no matter how spiritually connected we are, it is important to remain grounded in the body. We are, after all, physical creatures. It is the body, which keeps us safe and sane during esoteric and shamanic work. He grasps the second pentacle at the heart center. The star itself is a talismanic figure, the corners suggest head, two arms, and two legs. It is the magic, springing from heart-forward decisions. His two feet are rooted in the magic of the pentacles. It reminds you that you are protected from those who might you harm by staying grounded. Loosen up to move freely in any direction you like.

FIVE OF PENTACLES

"The ups and downs of relationships."

Key: Rocky road, Serious issues, Unimaginative, Struggle, Hardship.
Reversed: Dissonance, Bankruptcy.

The Five of Pentacles appears to reflect the ups and downs of long-term relationships, marriages, friendships, and the tumultuous nature of parenting. It is the darkest of night. A couple moves through a crisp winter snowscape. A woman draws her scarf close to her neck. A fellow leans on crutches with a bell around his neck. He looks at you as if in pain. A glowing stained glass window is above them.

The Five of Pentacles reflects the "Dark night of the soul." It feels as if you are entrenched in troubles and insurmountable challenge lay ahead. All appears lost. Yet, this moment of angst and anguish is not faced by the solo traveler but by a pair. This is the card of challenges faced together.

Pentacles symbolize money. The Five of Pentacles appear to warn of financial hardship and investment mismanagement. For long-term relationships it marks the nature of the couple's financial conflicts. Issues of spending and saving, budgets and financial indiscretions prevail.

The Five of Pentacles will appear to mark those moments you feel like an outcast. It marks being excluded by friends or social groups. This is particularly painful, as humans are hardwired to be social creatures. Research shows exclusion lights up the same part of our brain that feels physical pain. This is why being left out and being rejected hurts. There are times when you must move on from friends and colleagues. It may not be easy or feel good but the act of leaving is essential for your own physical and mental health.

The stained glass windows of the chapel are lit with ephemeral glow. The salvation the couple seeks is right there behind the wall. Will they see it? Can you turn to find the very thing that might save you? You see the answer but will you accept it? The glowing light also reminds you all is not lost. Safety, satisfaction and a sense of belonging will once again be yours.

SIX OF PENTACLES

"Ability to give and receive."

Key: Charity, Allowance, Benefit, Wanting, Subsidy.
Reversed: Envious, Grabby.

The Six of Pentacles reflect moments of giving and receiving. Gifts are resources, which can be recorded, weighted, and marked like an itemized list. Because the nature of the material world is tangible, those things can be weighed. It might sometimes be used against you. The misappropriation of funds and resources appears to remind us that the physical world only shows us what is on the outside. It never speaks to what character lay on the inside. The moment something can be added up, it can be wielded, used to control and fall into misuse, judgment, and extreme ego enhancement. In this, case it's the nature of giving, its beneficial side and its shadow side.

The beggars kneel at the merchant's feet. It might make the merchant feel tall and strong. Yet the cloaked figures may wear a disguise. The one draped in blue has some sort of ticket or chit in his pocket. Who actually has the power?

Determine someone's character by the way they treat people who they do not think are "important." The Six of Pentacles reflects giving, donating, and helping less fortunate souls. The scales indicate the benefactor is keeping track of what he doles out. Reciprocity, the idea of give and take is implied here. Do you have an anterior motive when you give to others?

All of the Minor Arcana six cards carry implied separation and hierarchies between people. One figure towers over the rest. This can means separation, authority, and positions of power. It suggests a caste or social system whereby people are organized via external attributes. On the subtle level, the nature of the Minor Arcana plays out in the progression on the number, growing bigger, larger and closer to its final goal of complete manifestation in the ten. The number six connects to the Chariot card that rides forward to make his achievement. Know you are progressing and be mindful of your actions.

SEVEN OF PENTACLES

"Results are yielded and future decisions are required."

Key: Haggle, Bargain, Quarrel, Clear Conscience, Ingenuity.
Reversed: Financial Anxiety, Lending Expectations.

The Seven of Pentacles is a moment where your results are seen. Their appearance is not quite what you had expected. Whether they are good or bad, the card reflects us puzzling over our results. We never know how the things we pursue and put our time into will payoff. We can pursue romance with a particular person and once they are in your life you discover they were not at all what you expected. You can work very hard for a promotion or career recognition and once your goal is achieved you may be flummoxed about what direction to move in next. This card is a place of questioning, even if you are satisfied with your results. It is the moment you ask, "Where do I go from here?"

Seven pentacles tumble our of cultivated crops. A farmer leans on his garden tool. He pauses to reflect upon his work and thinks deeply upon what he should do next. A tendril reaches forth. Now is an ideal time to take stock, make assessments and reevaluate the path you've chosen. Re-examine motives and perceived outcomes. Can you do something better, quicker or more efficiently? There is more to come with lucky number seven. More will evolve. The question is, how to encourage an outcome closest to your highest ideal?

The Seven of Pentacles appears to remind us of the importance of the journey rather than the destination. It is easy to show results via material things, money, and possession yet the reward is not inside of things you can show off. Did you enjoy the process? Has it changed you? What have you learned and what was gained in those places only you have experienced? Here lay the true reward of what you put your efforts into. The grass may look greener on the other side of the fence, but you are the entire field.

EIGHT OF PENTACLES

"Pleasure of work and apprenticeship."

Key: Career, Work, Artistry, Talent, Diligence.
Reversed: Arrogance, Greediness.

An artisan works at his bench. He holds a mallet in his right hand, a carving implement in his right, and wears an apron. These are all rich Masonic symbols. Examples of his handiwork line the wooden wall next to him.

The Eight of Pentacles suggests pleasure in the work of your chosen field. It also reflects a willingness to take pride in your work as it is on display for all to see. A deeper dive into the card reflects the spiritual implications of devoting oneself to their work, which is why Masonic symbols permeate the card. One's chosen work or field of practice requires daily devotion. It is only be returning repeatedly to hone one's skills, to show up, regardless of the ebb and flow of emotion which separates artistry from sheer talent. Talent shows flashes of what is possible while true diligence reveals unparalleled pleasure and results.

Have you ever had the good fortune to walk into an artisan's shop while they were busy making whatever their special thing is? There are people who train their entire life to become a master of arts and crafts, from baking to glass blowing to card making. Walking into a shop such as this can feel like walking into a shimmering jewel box. It is an honor to behold someone whose entire life is devoted to a particular craft. While the card doesn't suggest you must be an actual artisan is suggests taking a serious and joyful approach to whatever you work toward.

A town appears in the distance. It is a foreign place, something in the background. You, the craftsman, are lost in your own world as if in a dream. The work we choose becomes our world, especially when we are immersed in it. The figure also appears to be upon a stage which begs the question, are you putting on a show? Are you pretending to work when others appear? Who and what are you working for? If you are working for others, be sure it is also working for you.

NINE OF PENTACLES

"Delight in solitude."

Key: Accomplishment, Security, Success, Insight, Judiciousness, Wealth.
Reversed: Misconduct, Secret Agenda.

The Nine of Pentacles is finding your true place. It is the house, home, and garden within you. The Nine of Pentacles implies luxury, wealth, and riches. It is beautiful, cherished objects not because they are status symbols, but because the craftsmanship is appreciated. It is the appreciation of simple beauty and the desire to surround oneself with comfort and love.

Inheritance is implied inside the vineyard. A manor house in the distance. European vineyards are often passed down through the generations. Therefore, the Nine of Pentacles reflects anything you inherit from your family. It could be your physical traits, personality, or even behaviors such as likes and dislikes. We can look at Pentacles in this card as the DNA we carry inside of us. To look back on those we came from helps us to find our place in the stream of life. It connects us as a link between those in the past and those in an unknowable future. It is in every sense our House of Spirits card.

The symbol of Venus decorates the figure's gown thus connecting her to the Empress card. It is the card of courtship and adoration as well as personal tastes and aesthetics but above all things pleasure. It reminds us that pleasure is ultimately in our own hands. Can you stop and focus on simple things, like the sun on your skin or the wind in your hair? Can you lose yourself by savoring the sweetness of a pear? Can you look with pleasure at the people in your life?

Her gloved hand and falcon imply loyalty. Falcon training takes time and dedication. Wall hangings show Persian falconers with birds on their wrists as far back as 1700 BC. It is working in tandem with the forces of nature. The snail says it is okay to go slow and take your time. Allow things to develop without rush. Bursting grapes denote the harvest and appreciating everything you have. The Nine of Pentacles serves as a strong reminder to work in tandem with the forces and assets of your life. It reminds you to appreciate things you already have rather than focusing on what you don't possess or what others appear to have.

TEN OF PENTACLES

"Enjoying everything the material world has to offer."

Key: Wealth, Family, Legacy, Security, Cycles, Generations.
Reversed: Loss, Disassociation.

The Ten of Pentacles reflects the culmination of everything in the material world. This is the card of completion, fullness and wealth. It is family and friends, house and home, animal and vegetable worlds at your disposal. It is also the end of a cycle suggesting there's not much further you can move at this point. It is time to enjoy what you have cultivated.

The card shows three generations, the grandparent, mother and father, child peeking around his mother's skirt and even the family dog. It shows wisdom of the past and the promise of the future. This is the only card of the deck to show a threshold, the inner and outer space of a doorway. Ten pentacles are suspended in the shape of the cabbalistic Tree of Life. It shows the mystical nature of the invisible world.

This card reflects the legacy you are crafting. What do you give to others and how do you fulfill the legacy, which was gifted to you? What are the privileges you enjoy? How do you lift others up with the gifts that have been bestowed to you?

The Ten of Pentacles reflects the culmination of an absolute masterpiece. Vivaldi's Four Seasons, Dante's Inferno, the Taj Mahal, or Macbeth. These works of art exist on the material level but bring us into the space of spiritual joy and acute happiness. They are often full of complexity, like the image on the Ten of Pentacles, but they transport us to a higher spiritual level.

This card reflects the aging process and the wisdom it brings. The old man may be looking back at the phases of his life rather than joining a family. He sees himself as the boy and man as if the card were projections of his imagination. In this sense the card can be used as contemplation for where you are now and what it took to get here. All your previous selves live inside you leaving their mark on your spirit. Light a candle and contemplate the marvel you are.

PAGE OF PENTACLES

"A studious youth."

Key: Purpose, Dedication, Study, Scholarship, Organization.
Reversed: Distraction, Sad News.

The Page of Pentacles is beguiled, fascinated, and entranced by everything in the material world. She studies butterflies, hops after crickets, and catches fireflies in glass jars on starlit nights. She follows her nose into candy shops and rummages through closets to play dress up. She'll make a life size playhouse out of tree branches, stones, and green moss in a single afternoon. Her eyes are watchful. Her imagination is curious. Nothing distracts her from earthly delight.

The Page of Pentacles is activated inside you while engaging in activities with the curiosity of youth. You lose all sense of time while exploring nature, lose yourself for hours lingering in a bookstore, and make a mess of the kitchen baking up luscious blueberry muffins. The Page of Pentacles is activated inside you when you throw yourself into a new course of study, a project, or class. She is alive inside you as you focus totally on what is in front of you, the ego slips away, and you enter the state of timelessness.

Page of Pentacles types can be observed at elementary and middle schools and at playgrounds around the world. They are your children, your nieces and nephews, the little ones you hear running, playing and laughing in your neighborhood on warm summer nights. You know you are looking at Page of Pentacles types when they reveal something new to you in a state of wonder. Pages have the ability to stop you in your tracks, jolt you out of your head, and show you something you've never seen or thought to look at before. The Page of Pentacles is the ideal student because once she is hooked on a subject or opens book, nothing will tear her away.

The Page holds a Pentacle in her hand like a talisman. It is an object having the power to influence feelings and actions. Her gift is that she makes magic with what surrounds her. The plowed field behind her is fertile and waiting for her to plant her seed. What action will you take? What does your curiosity want you to plant?

KNIGHT OF PENTACLES

"Slow and steady does the trick."

KNIGHT of PENTACLES.

Key: Useful, Responsible, Sensual, Interesting, Integrity.
Reversed: Idle, Careless.

The Knight of Pentacles is the expansive quality of heavy energy of Earth. He is a slow landslide of momentum gathering toward inevitable manifestation. He brings about needed and lasting change when it is needed. He is steady and thoughtful in all ways. He won't act quickly but when he does it has far reaching consequences. The Knight of Pentacles listens for things in unexpected places. He can sense what a person, place, or thing needs. Physicality is important to this sensual Knight. He is comfortable in his skin and bones but tends towards introversion preferring thoughtful days and quiet nights.

The Knight of Pentacles is activated when you act with care and examine all options before proceeding ahead. After all, he is the calmest knight of the deck and highly altruistic. He activates inside of you when you attend the worthy work of building things that help others. It is the ability to leave your mark on the world. It could be a garden, a house, foundation, or school. It might be your investment in other people via social or teaching work.

The Knight of Pentacles will often appear in your life as a slow and deliberate romantic suitor. The Pentacle in his hand is a gift. He might offer it to you. It might be something he gives back to the world through his talent and professional work. He is a careful financial planner. He is the farmer that feels the land to determine what he will plant. He is the medical intuitive or a talented masseuse who intuitively moves straight to the source of your pain.

The field behind the Knight of Pentacles reminds you that what you plant will grow. Nurturing energy brings all things to fruition if they are cared for. The gate of his horse suggests taking your time. There's no need to rush ahead. This knight's advice is to take things slow and steady. You will win the race but enjoy the ride.

QUEEN OF PENTACLES

"Goddess of the house and home."

Key: Good hearted, Generous, Security, Freedom, Sensate pleasure.
Reversed: Shallow, Vapid.

The Queen of Pentacles is the goddess of Earth. As such, she wields power over all that is seen, felt, and touched. Her grace is evident in sight, sound, and taste. Every physical thing is reflected in her eyes. She represents the beauty of the physical world. Beauty opens the spirit and the soul. Like laughter or prayer beauty is an in-road to altered consciousness. New, challenging, and unique forms of beauty take shape every day. These are the manifestation of the Queen of Pentacles.

The Queen of Pentacles is operational within you when you are decorating your home, shopping at the market, and cooking dinner. The Queen is there as you tidy and clean thus rearranging your personal energy. Theoretically, you rearrange your space and rearrange your world. The Queen of Pentacles is the ultimate homemaker, she's there as you chopping, slicing, and dicing dinner. She's you inner gardener, She oversees all acts of self-care. She operates over the entire spectrum of health and the body.

The Queen of Pentacles appears in others when you encounter them, an individual who dedicates themselves to the physical comfort. This nurturing quality shines through all acts from home renovation to helping little ones out with homework. She may run food pantries for the needy; organize gift drives and fundraisers. She is excellent at managing and raising money. She instructs classes on every imaginable topic and can be found working as an interior designer or architect.

The bunny placed on the card represents the fertility of all things. The Queen's gaze reflects her attitude of adoration and love. Her red cloak implies passion while her green veil marks manifestation. The yellow sky represents creativity. Her lush garden and flowers are symbols of abundance. She is the most protected of all Queens. She moves slowly and is aligned with the energy of earth. When she appears in a reading, your situation will evolve in its own delicious time.

KING OF PENTACLES

"The one with the golden touch."

Key: Builder, Brave, Business, Real estate, Financial freedom.
Reversed: Manipulative, Overbearing.

The King of Pentacles is the King of Earth who wields a seismic power. He consciously commands each and every molecule of manifestation on the earth. His energy reverberates through caves and caverns, he casts tectonic plates like runes. As the king of manifestation, his energy exists inside every growing and tactile object. He reminds us of the physical power we have over our bodies. He is a mirror reflecting how we are the ones who bring objects into our lives through the choices we make. He builds kingdoms and is the master of finance and security.

The King of Pentacles is activated in you when you take small steps toward accomplishing large goals or making changes in behavior. The smallest changes often usher the largest consequences. The King of Pentacles who is slow, methodical, and purposeful understands this perfectly. He will hang back while others rush foolishly ahead.

This King looms large, like a Viking, full of power, potency, and fecundity but he is not always a man of many words. Don't be fooled, his quick mind is always churning behind his observant eyes. His physical stature makes him ideal for arduous work including things like fire fighting, farming, and carpentry. He is the archetypal farmer or winemaker using years of experience and an authentic and intuitive knowledge of the land on which he works.

A bull's head, the symbol for Taurus, is a recurrent theme upon his throne." The bull, four of which are placed on the King's throne and one beneath his foot, are a symbol for Taurus. Bulls were often the sacrificial animal for early agricultural societies as they were highly valued and considered a meaningful offering to the gods. His frock is covered with grapes denoting history and legacy. The wall behind him expresses security. The buildings and city suggest commerce and wealth. He appears to spring from nature itself.

ACE OF WANDS

"Spark of energy."

Key: Energy, Passion, Originality, Font, Brilliance.
Reversed: Disappointment, Flare Out.

The Ace of Wands is a spark of fire in the darkness. The beginning of passion, obsession, and excitement. It is the impulse that makes your heart leap and fills you with a flush of energy. The Ace of Wands is what gets you out of bed – at four in the morning. It is what fills you with energy as your eyes flutter open. In the deepest sense, the Ace of Wands is the seed of the element of Fire inside of us. It is toe-curling longing. It is our blood passion. Our hunger. It is the suit of career calling and spirituality. It is pure energy.

Imagine wandering lost through a dark forest. The trees close in around you, a storm approaching from the west, the wind picking up around you. It feels like watchful, hungry eyes are everywhere. You spy a light in the distance. You aren't sure who or what it is but it might be safety. It could be a warm fire, comforting food, and a soft bed. It could even be danger but it doesn't matter. The light fills you with hope and it draws you close. You move toward it. The Ace of Wands is what gives you a focus point when you have no place left to turn.

The Wand energy is powerful. It can nurture and warm when used safely. It will singe if you move too fast or too close. It incinerates like a wildfire if used care-lessly. The Ace of Wands carries the potential to engulf, devour, and incinerate everything if not contained. It is the internal fire that yogis stoke during their practice. It is the spirit felt by pulpit preachers spouting fire and brimstone. It is the combustible, unavoidable element making life worth living, gets us all into trouble, and defines who we are.

When the Ace of Wands appears in a reading it suggests vitality and excitement. It is a call you must answer and you have the willpower to do it. It is originality and creativity. Take a risk. Take action now. Don't look back. The path is unfolding before you. Let the Ace of Wands light your way.

TWO OF WANDS

"Make a plan."

Key: Visions of the future, Split between worlds,
Material wealth without love, Duality.
Reversed: Unstable emotions, breakup.

The timing is ripe the time to plot and plan. Make alliances, list your goals, create a vision board, and write out your plan for action. The world is in your hands. The energy of fire brings you higher than you've ever been before. A view unfolds. The energy of passion swings in your favor. Business partnerships are favorable as people of equal verve and ideals are soon to be united. Like-minded people are drawn to you.

The Two of Wands marks a moment of clever daring. Hatch your plan but do not rush into action. Be sure to wait until the moment is just right. There is no such thing as luck. You've been preparing for this moment all your life. A well-executed plan culminates with a combination of passion, knowledge, and execution.

The Two of Wands emulates the Emperor card. The figure surveys a great expanse while holding a globe in one hand (the Emperor holds a globe) and a Wand in the other (the Emperor holds the ankh). It suggests being aware of the position you stand in. It is the ability to read the room and make your moves accordingly. The Emperor and the Two of Wands is adorned in fiery red and orange clothing. This signifies a smoldering and combustible energy. The red roses and white lilies recall the blossoming magic of the Magician card. Anything is possible when you put time and energy into it.

This is the moment in which personal power is realized and recognized. Wands light us up and now we contemplate the direction we will move forward in. It is exciting in the sense that anything is possible. You know what you are holding has the potential to change everything.

The reversal of the Two of Wands reflects an inability to trust in oneself and general feelings of awkwardness. The answer to these moments of doubt is to stay present with the discomfort without pushing it away. Doing so will allow the feelings to pass unobstructed. Then you will be free to move forward.

THREE OF WANDS

"Fortune favors the bold."

Key: Trade, Commerce, Putting one's ships to sea, Business ventures.
Reverse: Break from work.

You have established yourself as a force to be reckoned with. Now is the time to make your power moves. The Three of Wands is a card of expansion and creation. The sorceress has cast her spell, offerings are made, a prayer is whispered, the send button hit. Messages and communications are on the way. This card gathers people for collaborations, people are united for a common goal as in a party or political action. The fire has been stoked and it is burning bright. A clear connection exists between the Two and Three of Wands as if there were consecutive scenes in the same film. The Two of Wands suggested careful planning. The Three of Wands is the execution of that plan.

A figure faces a bay and shipping port. The illustration represents you gazing out at your playing field. If the world was a board game, you are making your move. Your hand is good. The figure stands between Wands which reflect standing inside of a nurturing passion that protects and sustains you. The flowering leaves depict growth and manifestation. Three ships are in the distance. These ships reflect your ideas moving forth. You are literally sending your ships out to sea and will continue to watch over them. It is too early to know what the ultimate results will be but it is enough to know you have put your plans into action.

There is cooperation among other in your plans. You have collaborators on your side and people are rooting for your success. You will find help and aid in your goals. Patrons appear, family members step up to offer you help and guidance. The energy of creativity unfolds as others are touched by your passion and vision. You inspire others with your actions. They are in awe of the guts and glory you display with ease. All aspects of this card are favorable.

FOUR OF WANDS

"A time to celebrate."

Key: Parties, Community, Pastoral Life, Sanctuary, Plentitude, Domestic Bliss.
Reversal: Same meaning as upright.

The Four of Wands represents stability in the realm of passion. It is a happy home, marriage, and celebration. It speaks of midsummer fertility magic and fire festivals. It signifies summer festivals, concerts, and revelry. It is a return to the natural world, being in touch with the earth when she is at the height of her powers. It is blooming and blossoming. Passionate stability is reflected by a fire that does not consume but cultivates. This card appears to show us how to have a plain old good time.

The Four of Wands is unique in that the Wands stand at the fore upon a stage. The humans are painted on the backdrop. In this sense, it shows you that people entering your life. The wands are arranged like a doorway or threshold. You can gaze into your future too see the goodness that is soon to arrive.

The human need to share feelings and enthusiasm is paramount in the Four of Wands. Joy is better shared with others than experienced alone. It is receiving good news and wanting to share it with others. It represents good fortune freely and with no strings attached. It is inspiring others by gifting them with the same things that have filled you with joy. In a practical sense, this card appears to suggest a trip into the countryside. It suggests time spent in nature among fields and forests. It is relaxing during the long lazy days of summer. Prosperity and peace reign.

Venus, which is the essence of love, is symbolized by the roses in the garland and in the bouquets of summer revelers. A distant bridge is a gateway to happiness and manifestation as evident in the foliage. The castle walls and manor house suggests the history of community and family. It is security and wealth. It is sharing family traditions and goals met. We heal the past when we influence the future with an energetic alignment. Sharing joy amplifies happiness and accomplishments.

FIVE OF WANDS

"People worked up as in a skirmish."

Key: False Fight, Struggle for Fortune, Battle of Life, Gain.
Reversed: Cheating, Shenanigans.

The Five of Wands reflects the energy of a crowd all fired up. Depending on surrounding cards the Five of Wands is infectious positive energy whereby people are excitedly bouncing ideas off one another. It is a work or sports team working together by fusing passion and stoking the flames of creativity and enterprise.

If darker cards surround the Five of Wands, it can reflect moments when family or the workplace is in complete disarray. It can feel like everyone is out for blood. The incendiary nature of this interaction is fire building, which will ultimately lead to combustion. This could evolve into dangerous situations. Crowds sometimes turn to violence. Peaceful protests become dangerous. Fights unexpectedly break out. It is also the point in a long-term relationship where the flames of desire are replaced with the intensity of anger. Fighting replaces intimacy.

The card displays five young figures. They each hold a Wand, which represents their idea or passion. Each figure takes a solid stance with their feet firmly on the ground. No one is ready to give in. The secret of this card is that if they work together their wands will form a five-pointed star. Thus, the magical nature of combined creativity unfolds.

Do you allow yourself to be open to the inspiration of others? It is important not to work in the vacuum of seclusion. Sharing energy builds upon what you have already constructed. Regardless of the lightness or darkness of this card, the most important take away is that our passionate beliefs have the ability to transform any situation. Encourage debate. Broaden your spectrum to include other's ideas. When passion turns to drama and people are worked up for no reason, step aside and move onward. Don't get wrapped up. Avoid distraction.

SIX OF WANDS

"Inspiring others through your actions."

Key: Triumphant victory, Stupendous news, Expectations, Parade.
Reversed: Enemy at the gate, Worthy opponent.

It is time to celebrate and enjoy recognition and adulation resulting from all your hard work. Good news leads to public admiration. You are riding high. It is the card of achievement, of reaching goals, and announcing victory. Don't stop now, more is to come. Sixes are never the end of a story. While more is sure to unfold you can take pleasure in the rewards you have earned thus far.

The Six of Wands reflects how others support your work and effort. It is often winning an award or some form of recognition. You've taken a risk. It pays off in spades. Following your true nature and deepest instincts has served you well. Others stand up and take notice. It is a reminder that when you are true to yourself, it shows other people how to do the same for themselves. The crowd cheers you because they see themselves in you. Passion is infectious.

A figure rides his horse in a procession and the wand with a victory wreath is an omen of the World card. Everything is soon to be at your fingertips. The horse gazes back into the past or even slyly at the reader. The stallion is covered by a green cloak covering some secret yet to be revealed. Five people march beside the horse and carry wands. They represent the support of people closest to you.

All sixes in the Minor Arcana reflect hierarchies. This differentiation appears in the Six of Wands between the height of the horse rider and the parade revelers. It can imply separation, authority, and positions of power. Do not get carried away by the recognition and stay humble in your effort. The number six also relates to the Chariot card, which is the card of moving steadily forward in the direction of your choosing.

The card's reversal can imply that someone has it out for you. It is the power of any and jealousy of others who covet your success. Those who bear the brunt of success and who stand as examples to others bear the responsibility for their actions. How do you hold yourself as an example? Can you point people in the direction of their own unique magic by avoiding the temptation of believing in the ego's myth of who you are?

SEVEN OF WANDS

"Defending your life."

Key: Advantageous position, Contentious negotiation, Untouchable, Defense.
Reversed: Decisions made in haste, Jitters.

Feeling a little defensive lately? The Seven of Wands suggests defending one's ground. You are fierce and quick to guard what is yours from those who want it. The card suggests court cases, fighting for equal rights, and political discussion spiraling away from healthy debate and into ornery arguments. It is the state of feeling personally challenged in a subject that means the world to you. Passions are inflamed to the degree that hot exchanges ensue.

A closer inspection of the card begs the question, are you fighting a fair fight or, like Don Quixote attacking windmills, creating something out of nothing? It is human nature to take other people's actions and words personally. We insert our ego into so many situations that have nothing to do with us. Are we giving others too much credit? Worse yet, are we giving them the power to distract us from the things that truly matter?

The card indicates that no matter the situation, you hold the upper ground. Do not rest assured. The outcomes are still undetermined. Do your best with the advantage you have earned. Make the most of it and move on as quickly as you can.

Observant readers will note the figure wears mismatching footwear. He dons a boot on his left foot and a shoe on his right. This implies a fast get-away as if he's grabbed his clothes and run like crazy out the door. Perhaps he was caught with a person he shouldn't have been with doing things that are better kept private? No matter, the cat is out of the bag. His shenanigans are on display for all to see.

An alternative reading of the Seven of Wands suggests that the figure is not fighting with the crowd below but igniting their torches with his own ideas and energy. In this case, he is like a preacher in the pulpit firing up his flock. He is the lead singer of a band igniting an arena with energy. It is you, inspiring those around you to take action. It is enlisting others to help in your cause.

EIGHT OF WANDS

"Messages of love and fortune are on the way."

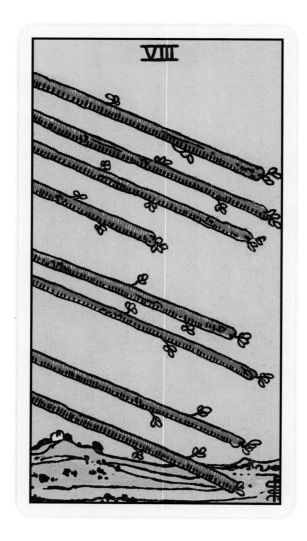

Key: Arrows of love, Speedy messages, Intentions, Bull's Eye.
Reversed: Arrows of Envy, Marital Dispute.

Eight Wands fly across the sky as if send by an archer's bow. They suggest hyper speed and rapidly unfolding events. Plans, ideas, directives are midway, like lightning bolts shooting across the sky. It is stealth precision and a visual reflection of your focused energy in action. This card governs all forms of communication from letter writing – to texts and emails. This card reminds you to make sure you are getting to message across to the person or people who need to hear it. It can also imply the helping hands you requested are on the way.

The Eight of Wands is the call and response of the universe. You make your wishes known through an invocation, spell, or simply saying what you want. The universe responds in what many call synchronicity or coincidence. Tarot readers know this is actually how we converse and communicate with the natural world acting in its own accord. Just as the Five of Swords reminds us to speak with kindness and care, so does the Eight of Wands remind us about the strength and power of our intentions.

There is a message in this card that reminds you the actions presented cannot be undone. The messages you have sent are out there. They will hit their mark. They carry ramifications. It is a reminder to think before you speak and act. Recall the karmic nature of the world. What you put out is always returned to the sender.

A house sits atop a hill suggesting matters pertaining to family and home life. A fertile land extends beneath the Wands suggesting the timing is ripe and the situation rosy. Rivers served as early roads and therefore imply transit and messages. The sky is a clear open blue reflecting creativity and clarity in your given situation. All systems signal go. To discover where the flying Wands are likely to land, flip another card. Place to the right of the Eight of Wands and interpret.

NINE OF WANDS

"Breaking past old barriers."

Key: Strong opponent, Formidable Antagonist, Detention, Strength in opposition.
Reversed: Stumbling block, Misfortune.

A figure stands upon a stage slyly looking around him as if to detect any nearby danger. He holds a Wand in hand as if he used it to move through the fence of Wands behind him. The Nine of Wands is about breaking barriers and moving into a new space. You have pushed yourself out of your comfort zone. New territory stands waiting to be explored. Possibilities you have never enjoyed before are available. Don't let it throw you just because it is new and unfamiliar. You'll soon become accustomed to it and move on to a new unknown frontier.

The Nine of Wands is the card of shattering a glass ceiling. It is taking energy reserves and moving into a space of transformation. It can reflect moving out of your parent's home, going off to college, or finally getting your own – apartment – sans roommates. It is a risk that pays off like bungee jumping or asking someone you admire out for coffee or a date. It is an action that has a real and true consequence in your life. It is the bravery to stick up for yourself in the place where you used to cower. It is an exciting creative experience where you see or do something completely new.

The bandage on the fellow's head is a reminder that every wound carries a lesson. You have been brave. What does not kill you truly does build character and makes you stronger. It marks you in visible and invisible ways. We bear a scar from an abusive relationship that taught us to be fierce and strong. Recovery from an addiction has taught us valuable lessons we would not know otherwise. We become more human, more alive with each challenge met.

The card echoes our need to move further, once one goal is attained. It is the nature of Wands and the element of fire to keep going. In many ways, Wands is the most exhaustive suit of Tarot. Remember to rest and not run the risk of burnout. This way, your inner fire will always create a pleasurable, long-lasting, slow burn.

TEN OF WANDS

"Putting down heavy burdens so a cycle can renew."

Key: Burdens of success and victory, Fortune bearing oppression.
Reversed: Conspiracies, Antithesis.

The Ten of Wands reflects a time for rest. Your energetic reserves are running low. You are done, finished, and you need a break. This card often reflects the toll hard work takes on the body, resulting in physical tiredness. It is time to stop moving. Give your body a rest.

Wands are the energizing suits, stoking our spirits, boiling our blood, and thrusting us into action. Wands, the essence of erotic love and passion, are the most electric suits of the Tarot. The incendiary nature of Wands can't burn forever. If it did it would breed deep soul exhaustion. The sheer tiredness of an individual ravaged by the suit of Wands is illustrated in the Ten of Wands.

A fellow walks with a gathering of ten Wands in his hand under a blue sky over a small estate, a plowed field and neat patches of trees. This is a visual reminder about all the Minor Arcana – these ten cards is where the entire suit culminates. They mark the results of your efforts and the end of the story. In the case of Wands, your original idea has had many incarnations. It is time to put everything down and regroup. Figure out what you can delegate to others. How can you lighten the load for yourself?

The figure's posture is bent, and he leans forward pressing his crown chakra into the Wands. His disconnection and misalignment is apparent. It suggests you have too many things to attend to. You must put down what is blinding you so you can see again. He is also walking away from a situation. What do you need to walk away from to save yourself?

PAGE OF WANDS

"Follow your delight."

PAGE of WANDS.

Key: Gathering of intelligence, Focused passion, Adventurous soul, Faithful lover.

Reversed: Rotten news, Telling tall tales.

The Page of Wands represents the attitude of fascination and excitement. The Page of Wands places her attention entirely on what thrills her. Let pleasure guide you where you need to go. The magic of attraction is impossible to dismiss. Stop holding back from all the things you want to do. Indulge in your obsessions. Honor them by focusing on them.

The Page of Wands appears in reading as a suggestion to focus on everything that thrills you. You will be always be tempted toward distraction. Keep bringing your attention to the things in life that flicker and dance for you. You know what tickles your fancy. Do more of it. Keep it in front of you.

A red flame protrudes from the page's hat. She is the youth of fire and as such reflects purity of passion in its primal stages. Think of what thrilled you as a child. What did you love more than anything? Where did your fascinations lie? Books, movies, shows? Were you enthralled by pets, animals, and nature? Did you scour night skies in search of life on other planets or UFO's? Did you crave adventure, bike riding, the wind in your hair?

This card appears to reflect people who are faithful to themselves. They will also be forever faithful to you. Just don't expect them to drop everything and come running the moment you call them. They operate on their own time schedule. Recognize that it has nothing to do with you and trust they will show up when it counts. This card reflects those you can trust and confide in. It is friends and family that are fun and vivacious. They light up a room when they enter. These are the fun friends you are most likely to get into trouble with. In the end, it is usually worth it.

The Page is placed in a desert landscape to remind you she is the daughter of fire. Her red sands reflect the dry expanses found in the expansive deserts of the Middle East. Yellow and black are lizard colors. Lizards are fire creatures. Red and orange are the colors of sand and leaping flames. Turn a new page and let her lead you to the destiny that was always yours.

KNIGHT OF WANDS

"Hot and hasty lover."

Key: Exodus, Stampede, Getaway, Young man, Outgoing.
Reversed: Harshness, Tumult.

The Knight of Wands represents an attitude of an outrageous boldness. He is the expansive and unrestrained explosiveness of fire. He represents unbridled and uncontrolled passion. Fire's momentum takes him forward. There is no time to stop and think. It is passion's heat coursing through the body. It is the exhilaration of romantic relationships. It is feelings of freedom, the open road, and the world in the palm of your hand. It is a thirst that cannot be quenched. Feelings of invincibility. An endorphin rush. Once the Knight of Wands is recognized, he and his powerful energy can be harnessed for your highest good.

His attitude works well when you need a shot of energy or must find the resources within you to do something important for yourself or another person. Access this energy when there is a big project in your life. He is useful when you have to push through a life event, a test, and a challenging conversation you've been putting off. He is the antidote to procrastination.

The Knight of Wands is activated when you book a last minute trip to an exotic destination or make any sort of impulsive moves. You'll harness this powerful energy when gathering strength and pushing through the end of a truly challenging task. He will help you get over the finish line and allow you to harness inner reserves of strength and dynamism.

Knight of Wands' unbridled reversed, energy will cause trouble if allowed to run unchecked. His dangerous energy will not waiting for the consent of their partner. He represents a person who is so consumed with their objective that they wind up burning others in the single-minded pursuit of their goal. Extreme Knight of Wands types have no filter. No one knows what they might say or do next. It is awkward.

The Knight of Wands is captivating to behold. Beware when he crosses your path. His incendiary nature grants him extraordinary charisma. He's fiery and impetuous. He glows from the inside out. It's flat out sexy. This extreme energy is honed and observed in athletes, sports figures, and actors who carry Knight of Wand traits. He is a romantic player on and off the field. You'll find him seducing many, sticking around for none.

QUEEN OF WANDS

"Brilliant center of attention."

Key: Charismatic woman, Ethical, Noble, Sincere, Welcoming, Successful enterprise.

Reversed: Exceptional, Accommodating.

The Queen of Wands reflects mature feminine passion with a deep understanding of itself. The Queen of Wands knows the inherent pleasure of owning vivacity rather than rushing forward in the flushed excitement of youth. It is the maturity and knowledge to cultivate one's passion at its highest level.

The art of cultivating passion is akin to any other discrimination and discernment. Once it is understood, it can be fully explored and experienced in limitless ways. The Queen of Wands feels and exudes passion in all its manifestations. She dances from ecstatic sexual love to spiritual ecstasy to an all-consuming love of family and friends. In addition to her own ownership of passion and pleasure, the Queen of Wands generates fire through her actions, devotion, and work. It is the ability to ignite anything you do with your personal spark.

When you hold Queen of Wands energy, everyone stops to takes notice of you. Actions toward others, devotion to your internal flame, and cultivation of inner gifts make you an unstoppable force. Step forward and execute your ideas proactively. Productivity is at an all-time high. Brainstorm for yourself and with others. Create action plans to move toward desires. Put out feelers for like-minded people and those who share your goals. Shop for supplies, gather what is needed, and lead by example.

The knowledge of what you love has the ability to transform the world and yourself. She is pure magnetism because she's in love with what she does. She takes cues from other Queens and so should you. What do you admire most about others? It will tell you something about yourself. Observe your own energy so you can utilize it during high points and nurture it when it is low. Plan important, ritualized activities to align with your power moments throughout the day. Let yourself be the center of attention.

The Queen of Wands has an ease of place because she owns everywhere she goes. She doesn't do this by staking her claim – drawing boundary lines. She owns every space by embracing what surrounds her. She aligns herself with the present moment and whatever came before her. She is not concerned with the past, by what's happened, or by what she has lost. She cares little for the future because she knows it is always out of reach. Instead, she dives deep into whatever is surroundings her in the present moment. This attention is key to both personal pleasure and outward magnetism.

The sunflower marks the Queen's fire energy while the black cat is symbolic of loyalty, magic, and charisma. The cat carries the message of aloofness. It is a look-but-don't touch quality. Her open stance is sensual in nature. Reversed, this card can reflect a consuming love of family and friends and putting all others ahead of your own needs.

KING OF WANDS

"Iconoclast and breaker of norms."

Key: Self respect, Genuine, Health, Fortitude, Reliable.
Reversed: Unrelenting in Goals.

The King of Wands is activated in you when taking a leadership position in a passion project. It is you when engaged in the act of sweet seduction. The Queen languishes and intermingles inside the mystery and savors the quality of intense energy, while the King has his eye set firmly on the goal. You see something you want and you dive after it. No games. Nothing held back. No fear. He states what he wants, why he wants it, and how he will get it. You embody the King of Wands when you do the same thing.

The King of Wands is the King of Fire. As such, he commands extraordinary powers. What would it mean to you to control the element of Fire? The King of Wands holds the power to heal and nurture or incinerate and destroy. He leads with burning emotion as the keeper of such power. His skin is hot to the touch. His personality is volatile. He is quick to anger but equally apt to dissolve into fits of delighted laughter. Once his sights are set on something, there is no stopping him.

King of Wand's energy is as spiritual as it is sexual. You'll encounter his type in the preacher men spouting fire and brimstone in their pulpit. The King of Wands is the guru inspiring his flock. The King of Wands is a rock star energizing and uniting thousands of fans in a stadium. He is a political hero leading people to freedom. Anyone who uses passion, fire, and spirit as their guiding flame embodies the King of Wands.

The dark side of the King of Wands is the personality consumed with their own aims at all costs. They incite violence against others. Volatility is the dangerous side of fire energy that burns so bright the person loses sight of who they are and what consequences their actions have. Waite points out the King of Wands, "connects with the symbol of the lion, emblazoned on the back of his throne." The Lion is a symbol for Leo along with strength and solar energy.

ACE OF SWORDS

"An excellent idea that should be followed up on."

Key: Success, Force, Intention, Crowing Achievement.
Reversed: Nailing it down.

The Ace of Swords represents an excellent idea. You already know the solution. The only thing left to do is take action on it. The Sword moves through a crown representing you being in alignment with your highest self. Boldly move forward on your plans. It is the swift and clever execution of a plan.

This card appears to reflects your intellectual instincts and sharp mental acuity. Your ideas are in line with where you want to be going. It is important to stay engaged and involved. You must challenge yourself in order to move to the next level. Find a person or thing that is on the same wavelength as you and let them inspire you to greater action. It might mean finding a like-minded community or seeking out a teacher. It may be time to enroll in a class or go back to school. The key to the Ace of Swords is taking what you know and making it sharper. Fresh thinking and expanded thoughts will open new avenues of possibility.

Swords tend to be the scariest cards in the deck because Swords and the element of air reflect the state of our mind. Our experience of the world depends on how we think about what we see and experience. Events play out and we construct and re-construct narratives around it. You have the ability to choose and change your thoughts.

Swords are tools that can be used to protect or to destroy. Traditionally, a figure with a sword pointing towards the sky implies channeling the highest thought. It reflects being alert and willing to take the "highest" action. This is a true power stance. However, all too often, we turn bright, brilliant swords on ourselves with negative self-talk, critical thinking, and nasty thought patterns. Slice through negativity by grasping and creating ideas about yourself that lift you up.

The clouds on the Aces reflect manifestation from the invisible to the visible world. The hand glows with radiance and divine inspiration. An olive branch hangs to the right of the crown and is a symbol of conciliation and goodwill. The palm branch hangs to the left and is a symbol of victory and triumph. You will be triumphant.

TWO OF SWORDS

"Meditation into inner realms."

Key: Equilibrium, Intimacy, Fearlessness, Soft heartedness, Harmony.
Reversed: Forgery, Treacherous.

The Two of Swords is place where you stop giving away everything that should be kept for yourself. This card is a gateway to your inner realms. It is blocking out the outer world and holding all intrusive things at bay. Move away from the distraction of others. Put aside their wants and needs from chores and children from needy friends to bossy co-workers. It marks the moment you stop comparing yourself to other people. Turn off social media; rebuff the invasive demands of technology, and culturally imposed ideals.

Twos reflect duality so this card means real problem solving. A female figure sits on a cement cube, She wears a white gown. Her feet rest flat on the floor. Her arms criss-cross across her chest and heart chakra. Her hands hold dual silver swords pointing to each corner of the card. She wears a white blindfold. A crescent moon, yellow with reflected solar light hangs at the top right. An inlet of water is painted on the scrim behind her.

The esoteric symbol of a blindfold marks the initiatory stage of a ritual or being "hoodwinked." The blindfold is placed to help the person move through their experience with a heightened sense. Once the blindfold is removed and the initiation over, she will see the world with a new set of eyes. Therefore, this card reflects those moments of deep internal understanding where the way you view the world is altered forever. Once your decision is made, there is no going back.

The backdrop of the card shows a still harbor with slight ripples across the top. The energy of the element of air and the nature of your thoughts can always be seen in how the water is affected by the atmosphere. In this case, the mind is calm. Fresh ideas fly across the surface of the water and your mind.

Her protective stance covers the heart chakra, the place of vulnerability. She purposely forms a barrier. It is a matter for the mind, not the heart. Do not open your energy to others right now. Now is time to keep things "close to the chest." The gray stage reflects the gray area found between two extremes, which are represented by dual swords. In a sense, the Two of Swords represents the High Priestess becoming aware of the forgotten knowledge of who she is. It is how you arrive at a new idea that only you can conceive of.

THREE OF SWORDS

"Love triangle."

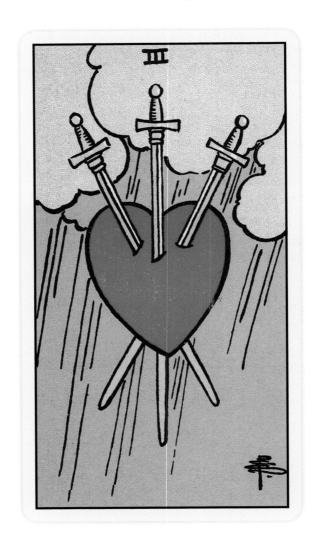

Key: Division, Affair, Treason, Heartbreak, Breach.
Reversed: Mental Withdrawal, Flaw.

The Three of Swords is the card of betrayal. It is a broken heart, a love triangle – and above all, three distinct elements ripping the heart to shreds. The Three of Swords represent more than romantic hardship. It's the fissures between parents and children, breakups and extreme disagreement inside a group of friends. Often, it marks you feeling like you are the victim of a stab wound. Someone has gone for your jugular. Your heart is literally breaking apart.

The Three of Swords reflects words, thought patterns and expression so the wounds are usually verbal. Upsetting news arrives, cruel words are spoken and the more you think about the issue, the deeper it hurts. The surgical perfection of the three swords demonstrates intentional pain making it all the harder to bear. This is a purposeful strike at the heart of who you are.

This card is truly the wound that lets the light in for we cannot grow if we don't allow ourselves to feel. Anything that opens us up is bound to hurt. Growth is never comfortable and none of us recover from love decimating the heart. Yet it is these broken bits that will reform. You will learn how to love better, become stronger, and breed compassion.

Christian iconography has long portrayed a sword through the Virgin Mary's heart as a symbol of contemplative compassion. In this way, the Three of Swords extends past our personal grievances and transgressions and becomes the place in which we feel compassion and heartache and despair for the state of the world. It is the horror and compassion of human tragedy. Famine, atrocity, war, and natural disasters.

Heartbreak is subjective and something we all must grapple with. Fear not, the storm clouds, thunder, and lightning, the drenching rain surrounding the heart will soon subside and depart. It is our darkest moments that carve our character. It encourages a personal evolution we would not have found otherwise. When the skies clear you will find yourself transformed forever. The Three of Swords is the wound that lets in the light.

FOUR OF SWORDS

"Thoughts in order."

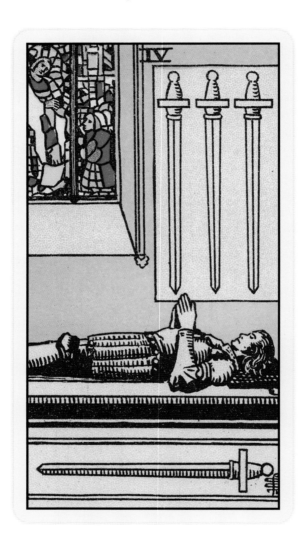

Key: Withdrawal, Seclusion, Isolation, Introspection, Rest.
Reversed: Care, Discretion.

The Four of Swords represents moments of deep slumber and evocative rest occurring within the quieting of the mind. It is stillness in its deepest sense. Listen to the quiet. Allow your mind's eye to enter the chapel of this resting knight. The pale yellow coffin supports a knight's effigy of rest, repose, and the calm throughout your inner sanctum. It suggests a slumber as rich as time and as deep as death. You can rest assured that all is well.

The chamber echoes with footsteps and bounce off of stone walls supporting a colorful stained glass window. Wisps of musky incense waft down from the ritual chamber. The window carries specific symbolism as a Christlike figure with a halo over his head and the word PAX embedded inside of it. The word Pax means "kiss of peace." It is traditionally bestowed to disciples and objects in the Christian Eucharist.

Three swords upon the wall point to three chakra points, the third eye chakra (intuition), the throat chakra (communication) and the solar plexus (love). It represents perfected alignment and the fourth sword supports and underlays it all. Indeed, the Four of Swords is a rest well earned. The card also draws parallels to Arthurian legends buried like secrets in European chapels. These chapels are often built on sacred sites of ancient pagan holy grounds.

When this card appears, you can rest easy about any decisions you have recently made. The idea that first sprouted in the Ace of Swords has taken root and has grown. It is a stable and workable plan and solid foundational thinking. Now is the time for rest as you prepare to move to the next level now that you've achieved success. Knowing something or being open to the unknown without question reflects a "sound mind and body." It is the purity of thought minus emotion. Dreams and ideals carry grand emotions. All too often in waking life we confuse our feelings for thoughts and thoughts for emotions. Go easy on yourself.

FIVE OF SWORDS

"Taking unfair advantage of another."

Key: Humiliation, Havoc, Scandal, Failure, Defeat. Cruelty.
Reversed: Funeral, Lay to rest.

The Five of Swords is the ultimate drama card. A wicked, unfair fight has broken out. A clear winner, loser, and mediator are seen. The consequences are real, events are set in motion, and sentiments are made. Words are spoken and they can't be taken back. Perhaps, you were too truthful or purposefully cruel? Maybe you were the victim of aggression. The group nature of this card also refers to bullying and people ganging up on one another. The man collecting the swords clearly holds a devilish advantage. He, like an archetypal evil villain, takes pleasure in what is stolen. He enjoys the force he administered and appears to savor the pain he caused another.

The Five of Swords represents a sticky situation reminding you of the power of your words. It is the impact of language on others and on you. It reminds you that words have consequences, especially nasty ones. The smallest figure in the background foreshadows the despair with their face in hands like the figure inside the Nine of Swords. The water's surface and background clouds reflect an agitated, wild energy. It seems anything could happen. The karmic implications of the card remind us how aggressive acts will return to haunt the sender. The card takes place on a stage. Have you recently participated in a drama for the public spectacle of it?

The Five of Swords speaks of adult "victim complex" issues. It asks you to examine the areas in your life where you feel as if you have been treated unfairly. What was your role in the situation? Is it happening right now or is a past event still haunting you? Are you in a cycle of perpetual disappointment and dissatisfaction? It may be high time you reevaluate your adult role in life. What do you give to others and what do you unfairly expect back? Could you be creating vicious cycles of abuse? The shadow side emerges when the victim becomes the abuser. The two are not separate. Acknowledge how you may have played both roles. Be willing to walk away. The best way to stop a war is not to participate in it.

SIX OF SWORDS

"Better times lie ahead."

Key: Emissary, Passage, Dispatch, Itinerary, and Voyage by Water.
Reversed: Confessions of Love.

The Six of Swords is a literal or figurative journey card. You are moving onward. It is the purchase of a new home or relocation to a new city, state, or country. It suggests traveling and vacations, which are sorely needed for healing as well as pleasure. The Six of Swords is one of many traveling cards. It includes a mother and child who suggests this journey begins with loved ones. You will not travel alone. The boatman can reflect a second individual with an emotional or financial investment in your situation. If you could escape right now, who would you take with you?

The card implies that "better times lie ahead." The rippled water on the right of the boat and the smooth water on the left suggest a transition from trouble times to smooth sailing. The depth of the water reflects the emotional depths of the relationship.

In a mythic sense, the card represents otherworldly journeys to the underworld, netherworld, or otherworld. Greek ferryman Charon transported dead souls over the River Styx as they prepare to enter Hades, the land of the dead. Ancient burial rites placed coins in the mouths of the dead. Archaeologists believe it was meant as payment for passage into the afterlife. What is the price you must pay?

All of the Minor Arcana six cards reflect the graphic nature of separation and hierarchies between people. One figure towers over the rest. It suggests authority, positions of power, and psychic energy moving between people. All the figures in the Six of Swords are facing away from the reader. In a spread, the following card will provide an indication of where you are moving.

Six swords are stuck like prison bars at the front of the boat suggesting troublesome thoughts are stuck at the forefront of the mind. A distant shore is seen. It suggests you are heading towards new horizon. The weather is calm and suggests a speedy departure. The ferryman's posture echoes the Magician's as a reminder of how you channel energy. It is also the power you have to change or adapt to any situation. No matter what anyone around you says, you metaphorically move ahead into new territory.

SEVEN OF SWORDS

"Making a break for it."

Key: Ambition, Goal, Nerve, Brashness, Uncertain plan.
Reversed: Sound advice, Warning.

The Seven of Swords appears to tell you is time to make a quick getaway. It reflects those moments when you want to cut your losses, take only what you need, and get out of town. It is literally leaving what you don't need behind you.

The figure tiptoes away with five swords, as sharp as deception, in his hands. His gait suggests you should take a stealth approach. Do not share your plans with others. Be precise. Get out. Walk away. His posture faces three directions. His feet move to the left, which is the future. His chest is centered reflecting the present. He looks back and to the right as if to check if anyone follows him. This suggesting looking back into the past. From the reader's point of view, he moves from the future into the past because we read from left to right. It is a reminder that our experience of time is subjective.

The Seven of Swords can be understood as "editing." It is the action of removing what is no longer needed. This may equate to cleaning out your closet and de-cluttering your home. It might mean you provoke a life-changing event by ridding yourself of old habits and discarding what no longer serves you. You may choose to let certain people in your life go by releasing attachment or expectation. Bright yellow permeates the card suggesting a high degree of creativity.

Festive, open carnival tents stand in the background. Cheerful flapping flags top the tents like cherries. A gathering of individuals huddles near a smoky camp-fire in the distance. It suggests taking a stand, moving on, without the validation or opinion of others. You may be finished checking in or seeking approval from others. At the same time, you may feel timid and have the instinct to hide your actions. Perhaps you will surface once your deed is done? In all matters, this card suggests you move quietly, without fuss, or fanfare. Not everything you do need to be broadcast. Your own approval and sense of self-worth is most important thing you can ever give to yourself.

EIGHT OF SWORDS

"Cocoon-like stasis."

Key: Horrid News, Disease, Blame, Crush, Thwart.
Reversed: Harass, Treason.

The Eight of Swords is the hostage-taking card. You are imprisoned by a domineering person, family member, or relationship. Or could you be held hostage by yourself? The card suggests culturally oppressive moral codes. It is the inability to express individuality. Your situation may feel extremely feels restrictive. The bills are piling up, you are faced with overwhelming confusion, or you feel like you have no good choices.

Like the Three of Swords, the Eight of Swords leaves little to the imagination. A woman is blindfolded and bound at the seashore. Her feet hover above a sandy and watery inlet. A fence of swords imprisons her. A turreted castle is visible atop looming cliffs. Clearly, the figure is in dire straits. Or is she?

An esoteric reading of this card suggests, like Two of Swords, that the blindfold signifies transformation. This is no prisoner but a person participating in a voluntary act of initiation. The initiate will see the beach with a different set of eyes when her blindfold is discarded. She is like the caterpillar in the cocoon undergoing transformation. The Swords are not a prison. They mark the boundaries of sacred ritualistic space. A sexual interpretation of this card (aligning with the Devil card) marks a proclivity for S & M, bondage, and control games.

The seashores are threshold space. It is where opposing planes of reality meet, sand and sea, field and forest. It represents those places where we can instigate great changes and metamorphosis if we so choose.

The number eight implies infinity. Swords represent the mind. Placing the two qualities together we discover the Eight of Swords reflects infinity of the mind. This is a never-ending intelligence available to you at all times. In this reading, the figure challenges her to expand and open the way she uses her thoughts. It is the power to conceive of our life and gifts. It is a life renewed and evolved every day. Our cosmic blot of energy and intentions radiate outward forever. We are the butterfly effect reaching out with thoughts forever touching the universe.

NINE OF SWORDS

"Vicious thought cycle."

Key: Bereavement, Collapse, Misfire, Craftiness, Hypocrisy.
Reversed: Captivity, Humiliation.

The Nine of Swords is a card of intense despair. It is the "dark night of the soul." It represents the gloomy and destructive thought circles in your head. You feel powerless to stop hosting them. It is insomnia, being wide-awake at 4:30 am with an alarm set for 6:30am. This is the headspace where you beat yourself up, chide personal actions, and second-guess everything you said and did. Those times when we hyperfocused on passive-aggressive situations and people. At its worst, it reflects holding yourself to an impossible standard.

An imperiled woman sits up in bed. It is the location of intimacy and restoration destroyed. Her head rests in her two hands. This suggests there is something you are not looking at. Nine swords are stacked next to her in darkness. They form a ladder she could use to climb up and out of her situation. What is your escape hatch? Her hair is as white as her gown. It suggests a sudden fright as if she's seen a ghost or suffered a night terror.

A colorful quilt covers her legs and a scene is carved onto her simple wooden bed. The blanket is embroidered with forty-two squares. Twenty-one of the squares bear the red rose of Rosicrucianism. The other half bears a random scattering of zodiac and planetary symbols. Moving across as one would read a book from left to right, the symbols are: Mars, Taurus, Cancer, Pisces, Gemini, Leo, Virgo, Scorpio, Moon, Saturn, Aries, Saturn, Sagittarius, Leo, Mars, Aquarius (partial), Mercury, Sun, Gemini, Libra, Jupiter, Pisces, Taurus (partially concealed).

The Nine of Swords appears in a reading and we are reminded to treat ourselves with kindness and compassion instead judgment and criticism. It is truly being lost inside the ravages of the mind. But to sit up, uncover her eyes, and consider problems by the light of day we can see those thoughts for what they are. Troubling specters of the unconscious that once acknowledged can be placed aside. Breathe and find yourself once again.

TEN OF SWORDS

"The end of a story."

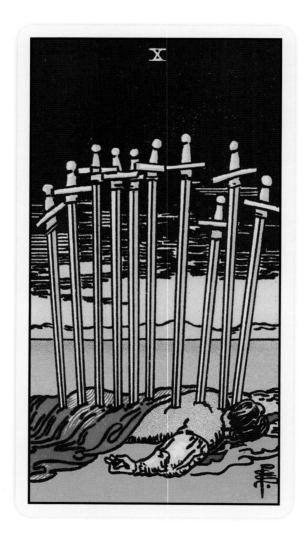

Key: Misery, Mutilation, Bleakness, Not always card of violent death.
Reversed: Blessing, Earnings.

A man stabbed with ten swords lay on the ground. It suggests death and destruction. Everything is finished. Or is it? Swords represent the mind and when the Ten of Swords appears, the mind is made up, finished thinking, and unchanging. In many ways, this card reflects everything we cannot change about others, the actions, opinions and morals of other people. Yet, the suit of Swords is a reminder of the individual power of the mind; we are free every second to choose our thoughts. Even if events or others can't be altered or influenced, we can change how we approach the task at hand or way we react to unalterable events.

Dawn pushes up against a black night sky and gray clouds. It is symbolic code for the Golden Dawn, which was the secret magical society, which the Rider Waite Smith Tarot deck sprang from. A golden dawn is the bright, shimmering beginning to a new day. The Ten of Swords suggests the worst is over. Since swords reflect the mind it is a mental turmoil that is finally vanquished. Tens suggest the ending of a cycle or story.

Ten silver swords pierce his spine, neck, and face. They make the card look like the ending of a Shakespearean revenge play. While these plays depict violent murder, cannibalism, and spectacle a deeper look into the card reveals the swords are plunged perfectly along his spine. It suggests spinal alignment, concentrated chakra work, and acupuncture.

The figure's hand gesture is the same as the Hierophant's. It is a sign of benediction. This blessing is always made with the right hand and with the last two fingers curled down. The gesture appears in early Byzantine art. A subversive reading of this image suggests that the speared figure could be the Hierophant. This reading implies old religions and systems are dead. At last we see that the Ten of Swords reflects the ephemeral nature of life. That nothing in this world lasts. Nothing is forever.

PAGE OF SWORDS

"Reading between the lines to discover the truth."

Key: Surveillance, Shepherd, Diligence, Probe, Experiment.
Reversed: Nefarious, Spook.

The Page of Sword carries the youthful and curious qualities of air. Her age suggests impressionability, fascination, and a willingness to play and experiment. Air is the element of the intellect and she carries a laser-like perception. New ideas and clues take hold and she will follow them through until the rightful conclusion. She trusts her instincts and pays less attention to what people say and more attention to what people actually do.

The Page of Swords reflects you when you are reading between the lines. She appears to let you know it's important to do so. She is the Nancy Drew archetype of Tarot. As such, nothing escapes her deep, searching mind. Call on her energy when piecing together the details of a situation. She represents you searching a person's history or historical research of any sort. This could be a computer search, research in libraries, or even going out to interview and talk with people to get to the truth.

You embody the Page of Swords when you are truly perplexed and intrigued by a situation. She is your thrill of the hunt whether you are after a bargain or playing after-dark hide and seek. The Page of Swords is super smart. She's the typical straight-A student who holds herself to high standards. She takes responsibilities seriously and reads voraciously. She has the uncanny ability to always find the right words and articulates truth clearly and succinctly. She is often found in libraries or solving a local neighborhood mystery. The Page of Swords can sometimes be a busy body that pokes her nose where it does not belong.

The Page of Sword's landscape reflects the quality via clouds and ragged high mountains. The ground looks as if it's moving under her feet, clouds tower behind her. Her hair flies in the wind and birds pass at high altitude marking her connection to the higher, wiser self. Waite describes her as "swift walking." Just as we can interpret energy by looking at the gait of a knight's horse, you can determine the speed of your current situation by her fast-footed action. The Page's movement suggests if swift action is taken, lightning fast results will appear.

KNIGHT OF SWORDS

"Act now, ask questions later."

Key: Full speed ahead, Accomplishment, Fearlessness, Indignation, Clash, Prowess.
Reversed: Foolishness, Squandering.

The sharp, expansive quality of air illuminates the Knight of Swords. The Knight of Swords is so carried away with his own ideas; he is often an unstoppable force. Cunning and decisive, this intense character will overtake you before you realize what is happening. His instinct for action overrides any second thought he may have. He cuts straight through to the heart of the matter at hand. His presence makes others sit up and take notice. People scatter, take cover when he appears like a tornado whipping up frenetic energy.

The Knight of Swords operates inside you the moment you rush to a person, place, or thing's defense. Acts of aggression are inspired by his attitude as well as unintended insensitivity toward other's feelings. He marks your need to exert control over any situation. He's also filled with tremendous courage and a willingness to risk without consequence.

The Knight of Swords can be a flash in the pan. He leaves as quickly as he appears, often, leaving people in confusion. His qualities can be shocking when discovered in others. His quick-talking and aggressive behavior can be hard to stomach. Romantically, he is the ultimate bad boy. He's a James Dean style, smooth talking, fast riding, fun-loving guy, who knows exactly the right thing to say in order to get what he wants. He might also be a valuable asset as the protector appearing just when you need him.

Waite calls him," Galahad on the Quest, dispersing the enemies thereof." No one will stand in his way. Knights reflect offerings, important messages, and their appearance marks the fluid energy of any situation. The Knight of Sword's horse moves at a breakneck pace reflecting hasty results in your situation. Waite describes him as "riding full course, as if he's scattering his enemies." Call on the Knight of Swords when you need to clear the room.

QUEEN OF SWORDS

"Expressing your mind."

Key: Articulation, Cleverness, Strength, Mental Acuity, Brilliant.
Reversed: Up-ended, Self-Sabotage.

The Queen of Swords expresses a mature and direct intelligence. The honest, articulate Queen of Swords speaks the heart of any situation. Her analysis is striking and rarely off the mark. She speaks the truth as she sees it. She reaches her hand out to those who approach. She is the feminine nature of intelligence. As so, she is extremely wise and to the point. She tosses distractions aside. The Queen of Swords knows how to organize herself and others. She energizes people who will work on her behalf toward a greater cause.

The Queen of Swords appears inside you when you keep the upper hand in an adverse situation with clarity and poise. She reflects anyone who owns their personal power. She also reflects you gaining strength of the mind. She is your trust in instinct and personal thought. Though she is clear, she is not cruel. The Queen of Swords is activated when a strategy is essential. She is you being your own best advocate.

The Queen of Swords appears as others who are a force to be reckoned with in your life. You may feel intimidated or inspired by Queen of Swords types. They take themselves and their work seriously. It may surprise you that they also carry a soft, sensitive side. Dedication to quality and truth mark these types.

Her professions include writer, editor, teacher, doctor. She is the brilliant psychologist and unbeatable lawyer. She keeps a full schedule, and checks off her to-do list with satisfaction. She's delighted to create a topic of discussion and is often one herself.

The Queen of Sword's crown and throne are decorated with butterflies, which are air and spirit symbols. Her cloak is dotted with clouds to match her alpine background. Her throne contains a cherub who appears above the waxing and waning moon. It suggests divine change is afoot. A bird flies above the Queen suggesting divine messages. Her posture emulates the Justice card. She always reminds you to express yourself.

KING OF SWORDS

"Suffer no fools."

KING of SWORDS.

Key: Military mind, Law, Judgment, Command, Power.
Reversed: Malevolent, Cruel Intentions

The King of Swords operates within you when working to meet a deadline. It is bold thinking, belief in task at hand, and focus. He represents having the utmost respect and owning your inner life. It is the ability to listen to the trembling inside of you and then making them known. He is a major authority figure. When you lay down rules and regulations, when you reprimand others, you are activating this King's attitude inside you. He's at work when you find just the right words to express yourself. It is that beautiful moment when you have the perfect response to any situation, especially an overwhelming one.

The King of Swords is the mature and masculine articulation of the mind. The inner workings of the King of Swords result in scientific and mathematic advancement. He is the nature and rule of law. He is the power of logic in the mind. Like the Queen of Swords, he carries a sensitive side rarely seen by those outside his inner circle. He states what he wants and has little patience until results are delivered. Above all things, he values truth and will stop at nothing in the pursuit of his goal.

The King of Swords will show up in your life as an older, "father figure" type. He is often found in military and strategic positions. He is often a scientist, doctor, lawyer, and psychologist. Waite claims the King of Swords contains the "power of life and death." He is quite an imposing figure whose throne is carved with butterflies. It is as if he is the masculine aspect of the Major Arcana's Justice card and the Queen of Swords is the feminine aspect. His sky matches the other Sword court cards and is filled with billowing clouds to match the activity of the mind.

CHAPTER FIVE

QUICK REFERENCES

CHEAT SHEET

There are two reasons why Cheat Sheets (pardon, we mean Quick References) can be very useful. The first is as for study. Cheat Sheets allows an extreme synthesis of the many nuances of Tarot. While they may be rough, they also can help the Reader to memorize the concepts at the core of each Arcana. In this regard, creating a Tarot Journal (see page 21), can be very helpful to slowly build your own cheat sheets and reference charts.

The second reason is to use during a Reading – especially for beginner Readers – when the information here can act as a cue to help both memory and intuition.

TAROT BASICS CHEAT SHEET

Elements: the four elemental suits connect to every aspect of life and the universe.

- Water/Cups = Feelings/Emotions: Art, ideas, and emotions. The kingdom of water rules our feelings. Emotions move and change as quickly as water. It is the transformative world of pain, joy, sorrow, love and every emotion in between.

- Earth/Pentacles = Materials/Things: The landscape of Elemental Earth: Imagine the feeling of the earth at your fingertips; crumbly dirt, smooth rock, freshly plowed fields, and vibrant mountains, trees, animals and people. Pentacles are all the items inside the material world, everything we can see, touch, smell, and taste. This world reflects all things (person, places, things) including money, goods, and resources.

- Fire/Wands = Action/Passion: Passion, drive, and excitement. Erotic sexuality. Personal callings and chosen careers. Spirituality, drive and our ultimate destiny. The fire propelling the energy of life.

- Air/Swords = Thoughts/Communication: Thoughts, ideas, and mental activity. The stories we tell ourselves, the narratives we create, and all forms of communication; written, verbal, and inferred.

Numbers: the ten numbers have each a meaning. Usually, Even numbers express stability, while Odd numbers express transformation and change.

1. One = Beginning
2. Two = Partnership
3. Three = Creativity
4. Four = Structure
5. Five = Challenge
6. Six = Heart Expansion
7. Seven = Uncanny
8. Eight = Infinite Perfection
9. Nine = Wish Fulfillment
10. Ten = Ending

TAROT STRUCTURE

Major Arcana: numbered from 0 (the Fool) to 21 (the World), they represent big moments, major life events and cross-cultural universal concepts (archetypes) like Innocent, Trickster, Mother, Father, Sage, Lovers, Death, Transformation, Mystery...

0. Fool – New cycles, beginnings, risk, adventure.
1. Magician – Action, awareness, power, charisma.
2. High Priestess – Intuition, inner knowledge, potential, authenticity.
3. Empress – Motherhood, nurturing, creativity, abundance.
4. Emperor – Structure, rules, form, shape, limits.
5. Hierophant – Teacher/mentor, dogma, belief, sacred space.
6. Lovers – Love, passion, eros, sexuality, choice.
7. Chariot – Victory, progress, will, mastery, movement.
8. Strength – Compassion, courage, self-control, fortitude.
9. Hermit – Introspection, spirituality, retreat, solitude.
10. Wheel of Fortune – Destiny, fate, fortune, turning point.
11. Justice – Work, law, karma, decisions, responsibility.
12. Hanged Man – Stasis, philosophy, surrender, mystic experience.
13. Death – Endings, resurrection, transition, evolution.
14. Temperance – Balance, duality, complexity, alchemy.
15. Devil – Addiction, control issues, deviance, greed, gluttony, slavery.
16. Tower – Destruction, release, catharsis, "Aha!" moment.
17. Star – Inspiration, hope, delight, clearing, artist/muse.
18. Moon – Mystery, dreams, psychic, strangeness, subconscious.
19. Sun – Expansion, growth, clarity, vitality.
20. Judgment – No going back, evolution, rebirth, awakening, highest calls.
21. World – Travel, completion, integration, highest self.

Minor Arcana: they represent everyday lessons, experiences and events. They are divided into four suits that refer to the four elemental worlds. They are divided in Numerals and Court Cards. The Numerals are in a sequence from 1 to 10. The Court Cards are divided in 4 ranks that echo the structure of a nuclear family (father, mother, older child, younger child).

Court Cards: they represent aspects of your personality, ways of approach and other people in your life.
- Page = Childlike awareness and curiosity.
- Knight = Expansive teen energy.
- Queen = Mature female compassion and nurturing.
- King = Mature masculine control and structure.

HOW TO READ TAROT

Reading: simple advice on how to read Tarot
- What catches your attention?
- Tell the story of what you see on the card.
- Choose a single symbol and interpret as an answer.
- What does a symbol mean to you?
- Read like you are telling a story to a child.
- Go with your first instinct.

Remember to:
- Center yourself.
- Call to your highest guidance/self.
- Ask for the information you need to be shown.

Powerful Questions:
- State personal responsibility.
- State the desired outcome.

QUICK REFERENCE SPREADS

Tarot Spreads: how many cards to draw, how to put them on the table, and what they mean. The procedure for a Tarot Spread is always the same.

1. Think of a question.
2. Decide on a Spread
2. Shuffle deck any way you like.
3. Draw the cards and place them face down.
4. Turn the cards (one by one or all together) and interpret them.

ONE CARD SPREAD (perfect daily spread)

1. What do I need to know?

THREE CARD SPREAD

1. Past
2. Present
3. Future

SHOULD/SHOULDN'T DO SPREAD (triangle shape)

1. My Situation
2. Shouldn't Do
3. Should Do

SASHA GRAHAM

Keywords: *Author, Artist, New Yorker*

Upright: Sasha Graham teaches and lectures around the world. Her work has been translated into Chinese, Italian, Russian, French, Spanish, Polish, and Portuguese. She is the author of *Tarot Diva, 365 Tarot Spreads, 365 Tarot Spells, Llewellyn's Complete Book of the Rider Waite Smith Tarot*, and the forthcoming *Magic of Tarot*. She served as editor and writer of Lo Scarabeo's *Tarot Fundamentals, Tarot Experience*, and *Tarot Compendium*. Sasha is a contributing author of *Llewellyn's Magical Almanac, 2020, 2022, 2023, Witches' Datebook 2022*, and *Llewellyn's Witches' Calendar, 2021, 2023*. Her tarot decks include *Tarot of Haunted House, Dark Wood Tarot* and the forthcoming *Tarot of the Witch's Garden*.

Reversed: On those less than productive days Sasha can be found watching reruns of Vampire Diaries, staring into the sky for hours on end and dreaming of far away places and adventures yet to unfold.

Sasha's evolving story (you might call it a fairy tale or a Tarot wild card) just goes to show you what happens when you push forward, follow your instincts, and believe in magic.